Open Licensing for Cultural Heritage

Open Licensing for Cultural Heritage

Gill Hamilton and Fred Saunderson

facet
publishing

© Gill Hamilton and Fred Saunderson 2017

Published by Facet Publishing
7 Ridgmount Street, London WC1E 7AE
www.facetpublishing.co.uk

Facet Publishing is wholly owned by CILIP: the Library and Information Association.

British Library Cataloguing in Publication Data
A catalogue record for this book is available from the British Library.

ISBN 978-1-78330-185-0 (paperback)
ISBN 978-1-78330-186-7 (hardback)
ISBN 978-1-78330-250-5 (e-book)

First published 2017

Text printed on FSC accredited material.

Typeset from author's files in 11/14pt Elegant Garamond and Myriad Pro by Flagholme Publishing Services.
Printed and made in Great Britain by CPI Group (UK) Ltd, Croydon, CR0 4YY.

Contents

List of figures and tables

Figures

Tables

Acknowledgements

First and foremost we'd like to thank our contributors Aude, Christy, Dafydd, Jason, Melissa, Merete and Neil for their wonderful case studies. We are most grateful for your time and hard work. Sharing your perspective of open licensing really makes the book. We owe you shortbread!

Thank you to the National Library of Scotland for being such a catalyst to this work and focus for much of our open licensing endeavours.

Thank you to the many colleagues who have shaped our thinking in terms of open licensing, and offered valued advice and encouragement along the way. In particular, thank you to: Professor Ewan Klein and Lorna Campbell at the University of Edinburgh; our former colleague and Scotland's first ever Wikipedian in Residence, Dr Ally Crockford; Daria Cybulska and Lucy Crompton-Reid at Wikimedia UK; Andrea Wallace and Ronan Deazley for their challenging and inspirational explorations of copyright and the digitisation of public domain works; the team at Europeana in The Hague; and the Members of Europeana Council.

Thank you to Damian and all the team at Facet Publishing for your help, support and wisdom.

Thank you to Gordon for tidying my unruly subordinate clauses and naughty split infinitives, and for keeping me fed and watered.

And finally, thank you to Katie for accommodating countless evenings of writing and for ensuring I was never long without a coffee and a brownie.

Gill Hamilton and Fred Saunderson

Disclaimer

This book is not legal advice and should not be construed as such.

About the authors

Editors

Gill Hamilton is Digital Access Manager at the National Library of Scotland where she leads on access to the Library's extensive digitised, licensed, born-digital and legal deposit digital collections. Gill has been engaged in open access activities at the Library since 2008 leading on initiatives such as openly sharing the Library collections to Flickr, YouTube and WikiCommons, distributing Library open metadata to third parties to improve access to the collections, working with colleagues to develop open licensing policies and recruiting and overseeing Scotland's two Wikipedians in Residence. Gill occasionally dabbles with linked open data and is an occasional Wikipedia editor. She is a Member of Council for Europeana, a member of Open Knowledge Scotland steering group, and a former Trustee of Wikimedia UK.

Fred Saunderson is Intellectual Property Specialist at the National Library of Scotland. Fred has responsibility for providing copyright advice, as well as co-ordinating licensing and reuse procedures. Fred chairs the Library's reuse and licensing group; he helped to introduce the Library's licensing policies, he oversees the Library's compliance with the Re-use of Public Sector Information Regulations ('PSI') and co-ordinates the Library's commitments to publishing open data. Externally, Fred is Chair of the Libraries and Archives Copyright Alliance (LACA), which is the main UK body lobbying for the library, information and archive professions and their users for fair practices in copyright. Fred has previously published on copyright in library collections and on the growth of the open data movement.

Contributors

Aude Charillon works as a Library and Information Officer at Newcastle Libraries. A large part of her role is within the Business and IP Centre Newcastle, managing the business collections and providing information and training relating to intellectual property to small businesses in the North East of England. She was part of the first cohort of Carnegie Library Lab Partners (2015–16), which allowed her to develop the project 'Commons are forever' at Newcastle Libraries, which aimed to empower members of the public about their rights to use copyright-free creative works and, in turn, to share what they create with others. Aude is an open culture advocate who is also interested in digital literacy, open data and online rights.

Jason Evans is the Wikimedian in Residence at the National Library of Wales. Jason works to advocate for open access within the culture sector by openly sharing library data and demonstrating the benefits to the organisation and the public. He has hosted dozens of Wikipedia 'Edit-a-thon' events and has managed a number of volunteer projects to enrich and reuse open access content. Jason is a regular contributor to digital heritage conferences with a particular interest in linked open data.

Christy Henshaw is the Digital Production Manager at Wellcome Collection in London, a free museum and library that aims to challenge the way people think about health by connecting science, medicine, life and art, through its public and academic outreach activities. She has managed digitisation programmes for the past 15 years, with a focus on historic collections. She leads the development and practice of copyright clearance procedures at Wellcome. Christy has a wealth of experience of putting these procedures into use as an integral part of a large-scale digitisation effort that aims to make digital resources freely available online.

Melissa Highton is Assistant Principal and Director of Learning, Teaching and Web Services at University of Edinburgh. Melissa leads services and projects in support of the University's strategic priorities for digital and distance learning on global platforms, blended learning, virtual learning environments, technology enhanced learning spaces, the digital student experience and use of the web for outreach and engagement. She works closely with academic teams to ensure that informed decisions are made with regard to publishing, sharing and reuse of content. Melissa has particular interests in digital skills, 21st-century curricula, open educational resources, research led teaching and online media.

Merete Sanderhoff is an art historian, working as Curator and Senior Advisor in the field of digital museum practice at SMK – Statens Museum for Kunst (the National Gallery of Denmark). Her work is centred on the potential for free access to and reuse of digitised cultural heritage. She is a frequent speaker and moderator at international digital heritage conferences, and has set the agenda for openness in the GLAM community with the conference series 'Sharing is Caring'. Merete has published substantial research in the area of digital museum practice, including the anthology *Sharing is Caring: Openness and Sharing in the Cultural Heritage Sector*. She is chair of the Europeana Network Association, and also serves on the OpenGLAM Advisory Board, and the Board of DIAS Digital Interactive Art Space.

Dafydd Tudur is Digital Access Manager at the National Library of Wales. His responsibilities include access to the Library's digital collections and services, and co-ordinating its presence on third party platforms. Dafydd has led on the Library's approach to open access for several years, forming its Intellectual Property Rights Policy in 2013 and appointing a Wikipedian in Residence in 2015. Dafydd is particularly interested in measuring the impact and value of open access both to the organisation directly and more widely. He also represents the National Library of Wales as a member of the Libraries and Archives Copyright Alliance (LACA).

Neil Wilson is Head of Collection Metadata at The British Library and has worked in a variety of library roles including service development, cataloguing and user support for over 30 years. His current role includes responsibilities for the British National Bibliography, The British Library's Collection Metadata strategy and bibliographic standards. He has led the British Library's work on open metadata since 2010 and represents The British Library and IFLA on several library standards and book trade supply chain bodies.

Chapter 1

Introduction

> Imagine a world in which every single person on the planet is given free
> access to the sum of all human knowledge. (Jimmy Wales[1])

This bold and challenging vision set out by Wikipedia's founder Jimmy Wales is
familiar to anyone working in libraries and cultural heritage. After all, we have
been providing exactly this sort of service for centuries by giving (in most cases)
free at the point of use access to our collections to people who visit our libraries,
archives, galleries and museums, whether at local, institutional or national level.
Many of the people who have over time benefited from this access have taken
what they have read, seen, experienced or learned and gone on to create new
knowledge, new art, new inventions and new discoveries. In this information
revolution that is the digital era, we can in new and significant ways extend our
reach beyond the physical constraints of our buildings and our analogue books,
manuscripts, maps, paintings and artefacts. We can today share our collections
with the wider, global world, thanks to innovations like digital photography, the
internet and the world wide web. To ensure that everyone who visits us digitally
has the same opportunities to use, learn from and be inspired by our resources as
those who visit us physically, we must endeavour to provide free and open access
to our digital collections. The tool for achieving this is open licensing. When we
apply open licences to our resources we ensure that cultural heritage
organisations continue to play a central role in supporting access to information
and knowledge at a global level. In doing so, organisations play their part in
turning Wales' imagined world of free universal access to all human knowledge
into reality.

This book will provide you with the insight, knowledge and confidence
necessary to implement an open licensing approach within a gallery, library,

archive or museum. The rewards of being open can be significant, and the costs and risks can be much lower than anticipated. Some of the biggest successes of modern communication and business, such as the internet and the world wide web, are derived from and based on being open. Openness, at its core, can expose the 'prior art' that sits within our collections. Being open can enable wider and deeper engagement with existing materials, in contrast to a traditional 'closed' approach where the ability to engage remains tied down through considerable legal restrictions, forcing interested users to turn away and limiting the potential impact of works. The greater reach and engagement with material that can be fostered through being open can in turn promote wider understanding and appreciation for these works, as well as for the role of cultural organisations in today's increasingly connected, fast-paced and open world. Taking an open approach with cultural heritage ensures that collections and the information that surrounds them, such as metadata and organisational documentation, are available under the lowest possible legal restrictions on safe use and reuse. Open licences are the vital tool to ensuring sustainable, secure and useful openness in cultural heritage.

The history of public engagement with cultural collections, such as those held in galleries, libraries, archives and museums (GLAM organisations), is old and rich in the UK and in Europe. The world's first national public museum, the British Museum, opened to all 'studious and curious persons' in London in 1753.[2] In 1811 the world's first purpose-built public art gallery, the Dulwich Picture Gallery, was established in the same city.[3] In 1824 the UK House of Commons purchased 38 pictures from John Julius Angerstein as the core of a new national collection 'for the enjoyment and education of all', which would become the National Gallery in Trafalgar Square.[4] Museums and galleries like these, along with establishments such as the British Library, the Library of Congress and countless smaller regional, local, educational and specialist museums, galleries, archives and libraries, attract millions of visitors every year. For example, between financial years 2004–5 and 2016–17 there were an average 42.5 million visits each year to the 15 major museums in England that are sponsored by the UK Department for Culture, Media and Sport, such as the British Museum and the National Gallery.[5]

Over the last 20 years, the cultural sectors and virtually every other sector have experienced the disruption of digital. Cultural heritage has a far greater ability to achieve core, foundational objectives because of the power of affordable digital technologies. When the National Gallery was established in the early 19th century, the ability of any person to engage with artworks (which had previously hung in exclusive, closed venues, civic buildings and grand homes) was exceptional. However, practical limitations required that anyone wishing to view the works of art had to travel to the Gallery's premises, first in Pall Mall and later in Trafalgar Square. Today, collections like those held in the National Gallery can be shared digitally with interested persons in central London, Manchester, Orkney, Moscow and Sydney, simultaneously, at low marginal cost, and with no risk of damage or harm to the physical works of art. The ability of cultural organisations to create and share high quality, safe, digital copies of works in their collections is viewed as fundamental a shift as the early establishment of public galleries and museums in the 19th century.

Europeana (www.europeana.eu/), the European digital cultural heritage platform, estimates that there are around 300 billion cultural objects in Europe, from paintings to books, photographs and statues. However, only 10% are estimated to be available digitally. Perhaps more surprising still, only a third of the digitally available 300 million resources are available online, and of those that are online a mere 3% are legally and technically available for creative use and reuse.[6] In an age of sharing, collaborating and huge digital potential, a woefully tiny fraction of Europe's cultural objects are openly reusable in digital form. Virtually all of Europe's cultural objects, 99.7% of them, currently are not.

This book presents the background to, case for, experiences of, and guide to implementing openness in cultural heritage, specifically through open licences, which are the key mechanism for ensuring that works can be used and reused legally. Cultural organisations exist in large part to ensure access to collections and to contribute to the preservation of past experiences, knowledge and ideas. The sector has absolutely grasped the value of digital to this underlying ethos, and millions of pounds, euros and dollars are poured into digitisation efforts every year. Today, with these investments increasingly established as de rigueur, we must think beyond providing passive access to culture. We now have the affordable and realistic means to enable active, engaged use and reuse of cultural material. However, if the cultural sector fails to ensure materials are usable and reusable, incredible potential will be lost. The ability to capture materials digitally and share cultural collections is a boon to the sector. 'New art rarely exists in isolation. Instead, new art is routinely built upon the creative work of artists who came before.'[7] GLAM organisations are the custodians of the prior art. The capacity to ensure that this prior art is shared, used and developed in the digital era, while original works and material can remain safe, protected and preserved, must be seen as essential.

In this work we elaborate our view that the use of open licences by cultural organisations is correct, safe and beneficial. Indeed, we argue that the converse – for cultural organisations to erect or defend potentially false, legal barriers to use and reuse – is counter-productive and short-sighted. Cultural materials that are open, through the proper and effective use of rights statements and open licences, have a higher potential for impact, are more widely available, and are more likely to contribute to further creativity, which is the bedrock of cultural heritage. In other words, being open should be part and parcel of a contemporary cultural or information organisation's work, and the proper use of open licences is key to this.

In Chapter 2 we take a historical perspective and explain how a 1950s US antitrust action, a persistent American Congressman, and a frustrated young software engineer separately laid the groundwork for the open movement. We outline how today's world of the internet, smart devices and the digital economy is underpinned by their actions, and how they unwittingly influenced others, leading to the development of open data, open education, open knowledge, open source, open access, open government and open licensing.

In Chapter 3 we look at the intellectual property environment and outline the role of copyright and other intellectual property rights, such as patents and trademarks. We describe the main intellectual property rights in the UK and Europe and discuss copyright licensing in detail. We explain key licensing terminology and provide a background to the most popular open licences, the suite of Creative Commons licences.

Moving on from these two areas of background information – on openness and intellectual property – in Chapter 4 we advance the case for the use of open licences in cultural heritage. We describe the benefits of an open approach – its impact, reach and onward creativity – and tackle head on the potential risks that are likely to be perceived from adopting an open approach, including the loss of income, visitors and position. We explain how these perceived risks can be avoided or mitigated, and make the case that the benefits of an open approach outweigh the risks.

At the centre of this book is a series of seven case studies from the Statens Museum for Kunst (the National Gallery of Denmark), the British Library, the National Library of Wales, Newcastle Libraries, the National Library of Scotland, the Wellcome Library and the University of Edinburgh. In these studies, contributors describe the various ways in which their organisations have used and benefited from open licensing, in areas including digitisation, metadata sharing, social collaboration and open education. These case studies provide tangible and helpful examples of how the principles and lessons set out in this book can be, and have been, realised in practice.

Following the case studies, we conclude with two chapters that provide practical advice on how to implement an open licensing approach in your organisation and realise maximum benefit. In the penultimate chapter we provide detailed, step by step guidance on how to make the case for and then implement open licences in cultural organisations. We address implementation from a policy perspective and from a procedural and technical perspective. The final chapter explains how to use and reuse openly licensed material, and how to distribute such resources widely to realise benefit. The chapter also provides some techniques for finding, sourcing and using openly licensed content.

Notes

1   Cited in Wikipedia, 'Welcome to Wikipedia', 2012,
    www.hks.harvard.edu/ocpa/cms/files/communications-program/
    communications-workshops/workshop-handouts/HO_SADOWSKI_2_
    Welcome_to_Wiki.pdf.
2   British Museum, British Museum – general history, 2017,
    www.britishmuseum.org/about_us/the_museums_story/general_history.aspx.
3   Dulwich Picture Gallery, About, 2017, www.dulwichpicturegallery.org.uk/about/.
4   National Gallery, About the Building, 2017,
    www.nationalgallery.org.uk/paintings/history/about-the-building/about-the-
    building.
5   Gov.UK, Museums and Galleries Monthly Visits, 2017,
    www.gov.uk/government/statistical-data-sets/museums-and-galleries-monthly-
    visits.
6   Europeana, Strategy 2020 update – Europeana, http://strategy2020.europeana.eu/.
7   Brown, M. A. and Crews, K. D., Control of Museum Art Images: the reach and
    limits of copyright and licensing, *SSRN Electronic Journal*, **820**, 2012.

Chapter 2

The open movement: its history and development

Introduction

This chapter explores the background, history and development of the open movement. It explains that the beginnings of the movement can be traced to the early days of digital computing and open source software, and that the role of free access to government information and the founding of the web have significantly influenced the movement. It looks at the history of open government, open access, open education, open data and organisations that advocate for openness.

Openly sharing our knowledge, experience, content and culture for free is not a new idea or concept. Sharing is an innate and natural part of our human character. We take this sharing for granted and most of the time pay it little attention. Take a moment to look and listen and you will see that you are completely surrounded by the products and outputs of our shared intelligence and experience:

- the building you are sitting in is based on architectural principles outlined by the ancient Greek architect and historian Vitruvius
- a child, friend or partner is excitedly telling you about their new idea to change the world as we know it
- the book or screen you are reading this text from is either a technology with its foundation in the invention of movable type or a modern semiconductor and LCD device – both capable of helping us, your authors, share with you what we know about open licensing.

Human endeavour is based on the exchange of information. To borrow from Sir Isaac Newton, we stand on the shoulders of those giants who shared before us.[1]

Of course, not all information sharing is open. We have legal frameworks, including copyright, patents and information security laws that limit or prevent the open exchange of information and content. These tools protect the intellectual property and data rights of creators, as well as individuals, organisations and nation states more broadly. The intellectual creations within this book are protected by UK copyright legislation, safeguarding our work as authors against copying, and limiting your ability to use and reuse our intellectual output without first seeking our permission.

The open movement describes a variety of loosely associated, interrelated and overlapping sub-movements, communities, initiatives and projects that have at their core the idea that data, information and content can and should be available to be 'freely used, modified, and shared by anyone for any purpose'.[2] This open approach is extolled by proponents as a catalyst for social, cultural and economic change and innovation. Openness, the argument goes, can improve government transparency, create new business opportunities, improve efficiency, and help derive solutions to social problems.

The movement is diverse, encompassing:

- the open source community and its development of software and applications
- open access and the publication of academic and research outputs
- open data and its move for wider use and interoperability of data
- open education with its ambition to provide high quality learning resources globally
- open government, driving for efficiency and trust through transparency
- open licensing to develop licences to support the various sub-strands and outputs of the open movement.

Numerous individuals, groups and organisations have played significant roles in influencing and driving the movement forward, including Jimmy Wales and Larry Sanger, the founders of Wikipedia; Sir Tim Berners-Lee, creator of the world wide web and the semantic web; Larry Lessig, James Boyle and Hal Abelson, the developers of Creative Commons; the Open Society Foundation and its role in funding the Budapest Open Access Initiative; and the industrialised nations of the group of eight (G8) highly industrialised nations through the Open Data Charter. Although the open movement has been advanced by these and other actors, the 'mother of the movement' is open source software.

Open source: the foundation of the open movement

Open source is software that is freely available with its source code, to be used or altered by anybody as they wish. Commonly the only restriction is that it cannot be charged for, that its free distribution should not be hindered, and that the work of others should be properly respected.[3]

The open movement originates from the nascent software industry that developed around the first generation of digital computers. A US antitrust action in 1956 that constrained the markets in which telecommunications companies could operate had the unintended consequence of causing the release of the first openly licensed software.[4] Ultimately, this drove the development of the first truly open licences and the evolution of the open source software movement. The idea of free reuse of the intellectual outputs of others was seized on by those outside the software sector, helping to bring about the wider open movement.

By today's standards, the digital computers of the 1950s were primitive, expensive and enormous in size. Only large organisations and businesses, such as those working in national security, defence and academia, could afford to purchase or lease them. Unlike our laptops, smartphones and tablets, these computers did not come pre-packaged with software applications. Instead, they were large boxes of crude digital electronics for which all instructions to manage internal hardware, code interpretation and process management had to be written from scratch. The task of independently creating these tools – what we now call operating systems – was difficult, complex and time consuming. Software engineers recognised that if they collaborated by sharing their code everyone would benefit from rapid and efficient software development. This culture of code sharing continued into and influenced the next generation of software engineers.

By the 1960s the cost of computing had plummeted and more organisations and individuals were becoming involved in software development. In 1969 Bell Telephone Laboratory engineers Ken Thompson and Dennis Ritchie began an experimental approach to building a new operating system. Their design methodology was to 'build small neat things'[5] or simple software components that could be combined to create large, flexible and powerful systems. This modular approach to software development now underpins all software engineering. Thompson and Ritchie's new operating system was called Unix. AT&T, Bell's parent company, applied a licence with few restrictions to this new system. The software came 'as is', no royalties or fees had to be paid to AT&T, no support or bug fixes were offered, and the licence allowed anyone to modify or extend Unix. AT&T's revolutionary licence for Unix is the foundation from which all open source software licensing evolved. However, this apparent generosity was not as a result of selfless altruism. Rather, it was a result of the 1956 antitrust consent decree, which prevented AT&T from operating in markets other than telephony, notably computing.

Low cost and the freedom to alter the code made Unix popular with universities and research institutes, where it was used for running computing facilities and training students in software engineering. In 1978 the University of California at Berkeley developed a derivative of Unix, the Berkeley Software Distribution (BSD; www.bsd.org), which was released under a similar open licence.[6] In the 1980s Berkeley received funding and support from the Defense Advanced Research Projects Agency (DARPA), the organisation responsible for constructing the early infrastructure of the internet, to develop and integrate internet communication and network protocols into BSD Unix. DARPA's decision to fund development of Unix to include the building blocks of the internet was a direct result of its open licence.

The significance of the 1956 consent decree that forced AT&T to license Unix openly cannot be understated. Without that open licence the late 20th and early 21st centuries may have looked very different. The internet would not necessarily have developed as it has, largely open and free. The open movement may never have been established. Giants of the internet age, such as Amazon and Google, would almost certainly not have developed. There would be no Android tablets or MacBook Pros.

The development of generic open licences

During the 1970s the software industry continued to evolve, moving away from the open and collaborative approach of the early years to become more closed and proprietary. This shift came about because the number of organisations and companies involved in computing increased. Businesses were making significant investments by purchasing expensive hardware, recruiting technical staff and employing teams of programmers to develop code and applications. Software was increasingly considered a valuable, core asset that businesses were reluctant to share freely for fear of competition. This led to companies seeking to exert greater control over the intellectual property in their software. Richard Stallman, an American software engineer, frustrated by these changes in the industry, announced that he would develop a new, free, open source operating system, playfully named using a recursive acronym, GNU (GNU's Not Unix). To license

GNU Stallman developed a generic open software licence, which went on to become the most commonly used open source licence in the world.[7] Stallman's generic approach influenced the development of other open licensing frameworks, including Creative Commons and the Open Government Licence.

While working at Massachusetts Institute of Technology (MIT) in the 1970s, Stallman, then a young software developer, grew tired of walking to the printer to find that his printouts had not completed because there had been a paper jam in the print job ahead of his. He decided to write a piece of code that would alert people to print jams so that they would be aware of the fault, and as a result help everyone save some shoe leather. He installed his code into the printer and everyone was happy – they could see when the printer had failed, resolve the issue and allow the printer to continue with all the remaining queued prints. However, when a new laser printer arrived, generously donated by Xerox, he was shocked to discover that he was prevented from integrating his print jam code because MIT had signed a non-disclosure agreement with Xerox.[8] Stallman believed that limiting access to the code in such a way was both unethical and antisocial. Recognition of this move towards greater proprietary licensing in software caused Stallman to develop GNU. To prevent his employers from attempting to gain rights to his code, he left MIT to pursue his ambition.

While writing GNU, Stallman examined and experimented with several traditional copyright licences, inverting them to create new licences that would encourage access to, and free distribution of, his code. In February 1989 he released GNU under the GNU General Public License, version 1 (GPL-1) via his not-for-profit corporation Free Software Foundation, which he had established four years earlier with the aim of protecting and supporting the development of GNU.[9] The philosophy behind GPL was that software released under the licence was free and open, while modifications and redistributions must be released under the same licence. The free access to code and the reciprocal nature of the GPL encouraged developers to examine the software, make improvements to it, and share their developments with others. This process helped to drive continuous improvement of GNU and software derived from it. The GPL remains one of the *de facto* licences for open source software, thanks to its strong popularity.[10]

AT&T, Thompson and Ritchie, Stallman and the University of California at Berkeley laid the foundations for open source and the open movement. Open source software has continued and grown. New operating systems, such as Linus Torvalds' Linux, have emerged and become integral, for example Google's Android operating system is based on Linux. Mozilla Foundation's open source

Firefox browser is one of the most popular in the world, tools such as SourceForge and GitHub help developers manage their open source projects, and companies all over the world rely on Unix or its variants for their success.

The web and the open movement

The World Wide Web is a distributed information service that was developed at CERN, the European Organization for Nuclear Research, Geneva, in the early 1990s. The Web is a large-scale distributed hypermedia system that is based on cooperating servers attached to a network, usually the internet, and allows access to 'documents' containing 'links'.[11]

The world wide web, a development which has profoundly changed how we communicate and access information, is another key driver in the development of the open movement that was only made possible because of open source software.

In 1989, Sir Tim Berners-Lee presented his employer, CERN, with his now famous proposal outlining the world wide web. Berners-Lee and his scientific colleagues were experiencing problems in sharing and exchanging information and documents because of the multitude of different computer systems at CERN. Data had to be copied between machines, or converted to different formats, or in the worst case rekeyed, all of which were inefficient methods that slowed the pace of research and discovery.

His paper, with the understated title 'Information Management: a proposal', suggested that by developing a suite of standardised protocols and combining them with the emerging hypertext technology, access to colleagues' information could be greatly improved.[12] Berners-Lee was given time to work on developing the core components of the web:

- Hypertext Markup Language (HTML), the language for encoding web documents
- Uniform Resource Locator (URL), the address of an information resource on the web
- Hypertext Transfer Protocol (HTTP), the means of retrieving and presenting a resource
- WorldWideWeb.app, the world's first web browser
- Hypertext Transfer Protocol Daemon (HTTPD), a web server hosting resources and delivering them via HTTP to the browser.

At the end of 1990 the first web document was made available at CERN and in

1991 others from outwith CERN were invited to participate. By 1993 Berners-Lee's colleagues recognised that what they had developed had enormous potential beyond CERN. If this was to be successful, the web developers at CERN realised that the underlying software should be usable for free, without the need to obtain permission. In April 1993, CERN released its web software into the public domain in the hope that its openness would encourage innovation, compatibility, collaboration and growth of the web.[13]

And the rest is history. Imagine if CERN had decided instead to limit access to Berners-Lee's creation: a world without the web? Today this seems inconceivable, unimaginable. The open systems and frameworks that the web was founded on have changed many facets of life inexorably: how business is conducted, how we entertain ourselves and how we socialise with each other. The web's interconnectedness and global reach has enabled like-minded people to 'discover' each other in ways that were not previously possible. People interested in the free and open exchange of ideas and content found, in the web, a new environment and community in which to work. Academics and researchers swiftly and openly shared the output of their work with their peers, driving forward the pace of research and changing the face of academic publishing. Educationalists developed courseware, tutorials and lessons, making these available on websites for others to use and build on. New, open collaborative communities established themselves and worked together to create products and services such as OpenStreetMap (https://www.openstreetmap.org/) and Wikipedia (https://en.wikipedia.org/). In 2015, the internet was the second largest economic contributor to the UK economy and internet-based activity accounted for 10% of the nation's gross domestic product.[14] All these innovations, connections and economic gains have been built on the open principles of the web.

Post-2000 and the major initiatives in the open movement

With the growing popularity of the web open initiatives in different fields began to develop and gain traction, including Creative Commons licences, open access publishing, open educational resources, open data, open government and the organisations that support the open approach.

Creative Commons

> *Creative Commons is a non-profit organization based in the US . . . it provides a simple method for authors to license works and through which users can determine whether a work can be used for specified purposes.*[15]

At the turn of this century, almost ten years after the creation of the revolutionary world wide web, there was still was no generic open licensing framework to support or enable open sharing of work. Creators could retain an all-rights-reserved copyright position, place works into the public domain (no rights reserved), develop specific, one-off licences to indicate how works may be used, or make works available with no statement about reuse, thereby causing uncertainty and ambiguity for others.

In early 2001 Lawrence Lessig, a lawyer and professor of legal studies, Hal Abelson, a professor of computing and electrical engineer at MIT, and Eric Eldred, a publisher and advocate of literacy, founded the not-for-profit Creative Commons. The goal of the organisation was to increase the number of creative works that could be shared, used, reused and redistributed legally by others. The founders recognised that there was no easy way for authors to express what rights they wanted to give away and what rights they wished to retain. Based on the spirit of Stallman's GNU General Public Licence, Lessig defined a suite of licences that enabled creators to indicate what rights they wanted to waive or reserve in their work. Version 1.0 of the Creative Commons licences were released in December 2002.

The licences proved to be so popular that 140 million works had been licensed by 2006 and by 2016 the number had grown to more than 1.2 billion.[16] The licences have been adopted across a wide range of sectors including in education, publishing, libraries and culture heritage, and used by collaborative digital media sharing services such as Flickr, YouTube and Wikimedia Commons, and by individual creators and authors.

Open education and open educational resources

Open Educational Resources (OER) are teaching, learning, and research resources that reside in the public domain or have been released under an intellectual property licence that permits their free use and repurposing by others. Open educational resources include full courses, course materials, modules, textbooks, streaming videos, tests, software, and any other tools, materials or techniques used to support access to knowledge.[17]

A brief history

Education is by its nature open. Teachers share their knowledge and experience with students and direct them towards resources that will help develop their understanding. With education accepted as a public good, we have seen learning and education progress from a privilege that only the wealthy could afford to a fundamental human right supported by the United Nations. Residents of developed nations are fortunate to have free and open access, without discrimination or exclusion, to education at primary and secondary levels. In many countries there is also 'open entry' to study at college and university through government schemes.

The term 'open education' has over time undergone many interpretations and adaptations. Its meaning no longer focuses on access to the educational system, but rather emphasises access to educational content, materials and teaching resources. This change in context came about in the 1990s when the tradition of educators sharing their knowledge collided with digital technologies and the web's distribution capabilities. This led to instructional and course materials such as texts, curriculum maps, images, audio and video being made freely and widely available on the internet for the benefit of students and other academics. Initially called 'learning objects' these resources were intended to be used by those undertaking independent learning, and by academics to use in their teaching, or as reusable components for the development of new course materials.

Leaders and innovators in the field of open education have varied, but a number of key organisations undertook early initiatives that went on to shape the movement. Three of these pioneers were the MIT and the Hewlett and Andrew W. Mellon foundations, both philanthropic organisations that support education. In 2001, MIT committed to publish all its teaching resources in electronic form under a non-commercial licence, unlocking access to knowledge and allowing anyone to use and repurpose the resources for education and research.[18] Recognising this initiative, the Hewlett and Andrew W. Mellon foundations provided MIT with an $11 million grant to establish and develop the OpenCourseWare website (https://ocw.mit.edu/).[19] In 2002 the prototype website was launched, providing open and free access to the teaching resources of 50 of MIT's undergraduate and postgraduate courses. The site gave access to lecture notes, examination papers, course outlines and other supporting resources. In 2017, materials from nearly 2500 courses are available on OpenCourseWare, with more than a billion page views per year, and many courses are translated into other languages.

Throughout the 2000s open education gathered global momentum. In 2005, the OpenCourseWare Consortium was established and institutions from around the world joined to work together to grow and share content, establish standards for access, interoperability and technology, and advocate for open educational resources. Another significant initiative of the decade was the founding of Khan

Academy by Sal Khan in 2006. The Academy grew out of Khan's online tutoring service and developed into a platform of mostly video-based open educational resources supporting learners across a range of topics. By 2017 it had grown to 20,000 video resources in several languages.[20]

In the UK, the development of open educational resources began with the Open University's OpenLearn (www.open.edu/openlearn/) in 2006, an initiative to make some of the University's teaching resources openly available. In 2007, the University of Nottingham established a similar service: U-Now.[21] The OER Pilot Programme funded by Jisc (Joint Information Systems Committee), one of the first national programmes of its kind, brought openly licensed learning materials to the mainstream in UK universities. The initial phase of the programme began in April 2009, with £5.7 million funding support from Jisc. The primary goals of the programme were to fund individual, institutional and subject-based projects that supported the release of large quantities of open educational resources material, and to consider and encourage long-term sustainability of these resources. The second phase of the pilot, running for a year from August 2010 with £5 million of support, focused on content release, use and discovery, and the behaviours observed in the use and reuse of content. In the third and final phase, which concluded in 2012, consideration was given to strategic and institutional policy issues to strengthen the general acceptance of open educational resources in UK higher education. Complementary projects ran in parallel, in areas including technical infrastructure, partnerships and content digitisation. As a result of the Pilot Programme, by 2013 open educational resources was well established in the UK and had become common educational practice in many universities and colleges.

Open educational resources and open licensing

In the early days of open education there was no standardised licensing framework for open educational resources and different institutions chose to license their content in different ways. It was common for academics to place resources into the public domain or to make them available without a licence, indicating the right to reuse within the material. Some initiatives used the Open Content or Open Publication licences that had been developed by the Open Content Project, initiated by Professor David Wiley of Brigham Young University, in the US. Many educators and institutions began adopting Creative Commons licences for their materials when launched in 2002. Today, Creative Commons is generally accepted as the *de facto* licensing framework for educational resources.[22]

Open government

Open government is a movement that places the transparency and accountability of governments at its core. Other objectives include increased citizen participation and engagement with government, economic development, and the stimulation of innovation.[23]

For much of the 20th century governments of most nation states were closed and often less than forthcoming in making information available and accessible to their citizens. This is perhaps understandable, given that the century witnessed two world wars, increased tensions between the West and the Soviet Union, the rise of nuclear weapons, and the threat of terrorism and disruption from factions such as the Irish Republican Army (IRA), Euskadi Ta Askatasuna (ETA) Basque separatist group, Baader-Meinhof Group and the Palestine Liberation Organisation. Given these tensions, it is in fact somewhat surprising that open government managed to gain a foothold.

John E. Moss, the open government champion

In the 1950s, the US was rife with anti-Communist McCarthyism. Many Americans working in government, education, trade unions and the entertainment industry found themselves accused, with little or no evidence, of being disloyal and participating in subversive, pro-Communist activities. Many lost their jobs; others were blacklisted and prevented from working. People were afraid to criticise or speak out against their government for fear of being called before and censured by the House Un-American Activities Committee. Into this environment of suspicion a young Democrat named John E. Moss was elected Congressman for California's 3rd congressional district in November 1952. Moss learned, while working on the House Post Office and Civil Service Commission, that nearly 3000 federal employees had been dismissed for security reasons. When Moss asked to see documentation relating to their sackings his request was refused and he was informed that he had no legal remit to obtain the information. Moss began to be lobbied by the press and media, which had experienced similar dead-ends in attempting to gain access to government information.[24]

In 1955 Moss became chair of the newly convened Government Information Subcommittee, whose remit related to 'issues concerning the creation, maintenance, and use of and access to Government information'.[25] Over the next ten years Moss conducted hearings into, and wrote reports on, the increased secrecy within government and the misuse of document classification that was causing many documents to be unnecessarily classified as confidential. Every federal agency that submitted evidence to Moss opposed his reforms. There were attempts to abolish his subcommittee by removing its funding, and the then Republican administration treated his work with suspicion.

During the Democratic presidencies of John F. Kennedy and Lyndon B. Johnson, the Republican party became increasingly interested in Moss's Freedom of Information Act (FOIA). Donald Rumsfeld, Republican congressman for Illinois, denounced the 'executive secrecy' of the Johnson administration and co-sponsored to Moss's FOIA bill in 1965. With Republican support the bill slowly progressed towards being passed by the House.[26] Eleven years after he started his work to improve the openness of the US government Moss's FOIA was signed into law on 4 July 1966. The act was groundbreaking. At the time, the only other countries with similar legislation were Sweden,[27] with openness written into its constitution since 1766, and Finland, with its 1951 act on publicity of official documents. Through Moss's commitment and persistence he was instrumental in establishing open government in the US and providing citizens, press and media with rights to access and scrutinise information on the activities and operations of the government.[28] Following this early example, freedom of information laws are increasingly common. For example, similar regulations have been put in place by Norway (1970), France (1978), the Netherlands (1980), Australia (1982), Canada (1983), Ireland (1997), the UK (2000) and Germany (2005).[29]

Open government in the early 21st century

United Kingdom

Up until the mid-19th century information, documentation and laws of the UK government were scattered across different organisations, sometimes held in poor conditions, inadequately catalogued, and in some instances discarded or destroyed. With the introduction of Public Record Office Act, 1838, the government sought to reform and rationalise record management into a single organisation, the Public Record Office, to 'keep safely the public records'. While the act ensured improved stewardship of the public record, it made no formal requirement for departments to provide the public with free access to information. Significant charges were levied on researchers wishing to access records. The act also did not resolve inconsistencies in 'closure' policies, whereby access to documents was prevented for a defined period of time. In the mid-19th century 'closure' was variously defined as indefinite, 100 years or 50 years.[30] The Public Record Office Act (1958) attempted to resolve some of the failings of the original 1838 act, addressing record retention and review, and reducing the period of 'closure' to a defined 50 years, after which records had to be opened to general public inspection unless special circumstances applied. The period of closure was subsequently reduced to 30 years by the Public Record Office Act (1967).

In 1997 the Labour government published a white paper, *Your Right To Know*, which proposed the introduction of a freedom of information act with the aim of encouraging more open and accountable government, modernising UK politics and developing a mutual trust between citizens and their government.[31] The Freedom of Information Act (2000) and the Freedom of Information (Scotland) Act (2002) provided UK citizens with their first statutory rights of access to information held by public bodies, such as central and local government, the health service, educational establishments and the police. The principles of openness set out in these laws were that everybody has a right to access official information, that disclosure of information should be the default position, that those requesting information do not have to give a reason for their request, and that those deciding not to supply information must justify why information cannot be shared.

While the UK FOI acts provided rights of access to information, they said little on access to data. In 2006, the Guardian newspaper began a campaign to lobby the UK government to make openly available the data that it and its agencies collected.[32] The newspaper argued that public data should be available for analysis and scrutiny since it was paid for from the public purse. The newspaper also argued that openness would lead to more transparency in government and drive innovative uses of data. In the same year, the Office of Fair Trading published a report that criticised the government for restricting access to data.[33] The report indicated that in some areas government departments and agencies were abusing their positions as data owners, acting in their own interests, and operating anti-competitive practices. The report also outlined that government data had a value of between £600 million and £1 billion and that this economic benefit was not being realised as there was limited access to it by the public.[34]

What followed was an effort to establish open access to government data. Much work and lobbying was undertaken in parliament, and input and support was notably received from Berners-Lee and Sir Nigel Shadbolt, Professor of Computing at University of Southampton. In January 2010 data.gov.uk was launched as the platform for accessing open government data. Datasets on the platform were released using the new Open Government Licence (see section 'The Open Government Licence' in Chapter 3).[35] Today data.gov.uk hosts thousands of datasets across most areas of government including finance, official statistics, the economy and the environment.

The European Union

Before the 1992 Maastricht Treaty on European Union (EU) the EU's policy style was technocratic and closed. Providing EU citizens with free and open access to official documents, information and data was neither permissible nor seen as a priority. The Protocol on the Privileges and Immunities of the European Communities, an annex to the Treaty of Rome (1956) that founded the grouping that is today the EU, stated that public access to the Union's archives was prohibited. However, a 1983 Council directive determined that the annex should be interpreted to mean that records should not be publicly available until 30 years after they were produced. The protocol's limitation on access reached beyond EU official documents, to the documents of member states. As a result, nations with a tradition of transparency, such as Denmark and the Netherlands, could not provide their citizens with access to government documents that related to EU decision making.

The EU faced increasing internal and external pressure to become more transparent and Declaration 17 of the Maastricht Treaty put measures in place to improve public access to information. The declaration required the EU to make available its policy plans and timetables, put in place processes for wider public consultation in policy making, and provide public access to information and documents when the interests of individuals, the public or the security or financial operation of the Union were not threatened.

In 1994, before joining the EU, Sweden made an official declaration recognising that the EU had made progress towards improving open access to official documents, but underlined its position that transparency in government was fundamental to the Swedish constitution. After its accession to the Union, Sweden, along with Denmark, continued to press for more transparency. The two member states accordingly set out proposals to improve access ahead of EU discussions over the Amsterdam Treaty (1997). As a result of Sweden and Denmark's influence, open access to EU documents was significantly improved in three areas: the principle of openness and transparency was written into the Treaty; the EU Council, when using its legislative powers, was required to make available all minutes, votes and statements regarding votes, thereby preventing the Council taking legal decisions in private; and the right of public access to official documents was introduced.[36]

In 2003, in a move to harmonise the rules by which member states made public sector information available to their citizens for use and reuse, the EU passed Council Directive 2003/98/EC, the so-called PSI Directive. It required member states to provide open access to public sector information at national, regional and local levels. In 2013, a revision to the original directive amended its scope requiring information generated by galleries, museums, archives and libraries to be made openly available (see Chapter 4). Although the public sector information directives did not address data directly, the EU Open Data Portal was launched in December 2012.

Global

In December 2008 a group of open data leaders met in Sebastopol, California, to agree the definition of and principles relating to open government data.[37] The eight principles that were agreed set out why and how governments, whether national, regional or local, should make their data available. The principles were used in the US to lobby for open access to government data. As a result, in his first day in office President Barack Obama's first executive order was the Memorandum on Transparency and Open Government. This directive committed the President's executive departments and agencies to 'an unprecedented level of openness in Government' and required them to take actions to implement the open government principles of transparency, participation and collaboration.[38]

The Open Government Partnership was established in September 2011 by Brazil, Indonesia, Mexico, Norway, Philippines, South Africa, UK and the US as an initiative to promote open government globally. It secures from governments that sign the Open Government Declaration a commitment to operate transparently, collaborate with and empower citizens, and use information technology to improve governance and fight corruption. To be eligible to join, countries are assessed against several criteria that test their level of openness and transparency including the availability and timely publication of fiscal accounts and budgets, public access to government documents and information, disclosure of the assets and interests of public officials, and engagement with citizens to encourage their participation in government. As of 2017, the partnership has grown to 75 countries.[39]

Open data

Open data is data that can be freely accessed, used, modified and shared by anyone for any purpose, subject only, at most, to the requirement to provide attribute and/or ShareAlike. Specifically open data will be legally open under a license that permits free access, use, reuse and redistribution, and be made available in a machine-readable format for free or at no more than the cost of its reproduction.[40]

The term 'open data' is used to cover a wide range of data, including open government data (ses section 'Open government', above), open science and research, geospatial, meteorological and linked open data. The open data idea began in the 1950s when the International Council of Science founded the World Data Center, a distributed global system designed to preserve and provide access to scientific data and documentation. Despite being in the early days of modern computing, the Council had the foresight to determine that wherever possible data should be made available in machine-readable formats.[41]

At this time neither the internet nor the web existed, so there was limited access to data resources for members of the public, and in general only academics, medical and educational practitioners and librarians had access to subject-specific resources. With the development of the web, the growth in computing power and faster communications, open data outputs have grown exponentially and been made available for consumption, use and reuse by the wider public, as well as researchers and data scientists.

Today the major sources of open data are national and local governments and their agencies. The scale of much of this data is vast, and commonly known as big data. For example, the Large Hadron Collider experiment at CERN generates more than 30 petabytes (30 million gigabytes) a year and the UK's 2011 census data from the Office for National Statistics amounts to 629 separate datasets.[42]

Linked open data

Linked open data is a particular type of open data that is formatted and structured in such a way that semantic relationships can be established between data. This linking ability is what Berners-Lee, James Hendler and Ora Lassila coined as the semantic web in 2001.[43] Linking data can lead to the creation of new insights and generation of new knowledge. Berners-Lee later specified a set of steps, known as the 5 Star Open Data Model, that explains how open data should be formatted and published in order to become linked open data:[44]

- 1 star – publish the data on the web in any format under an open licence
- 2 star – publish it in a structured format, such as in Microsoft Excel
- 3 star – publish it in a non-proprietary format, such as CSV
- 4 star – use uniform resource indicators so that others can link to your data
- 5 star – link your data to other data to give context.

Open access

> By 'open access' to [peer-reviewed research literature] we mean its free availability on the public internet, permitting any users to read, download, copy, distribute, print, search, or link to the full texts of these articles, crawl them for indexing, pass them as data to software, or use them for any other lawful purpose, without financial, legal, or technical barriers other than those inseparable from gaining access to the internet itself. The only constraint on reproduction and distribution, and the only role for copyright in this domain, should be to give authors control over the integrity of their work and the right to be properly acknowledged and cited.[45]

Foundations for the open access movement were laid during the 1960s, 1970s and 1980s. The traditional paper-based means of accessing scholarly literature was being challenged by increasing computing power and the rise in the use of the early internet. Content repositories such as the Education Research Information Center (ERIC)[46] and MEDLINE of the US National Library of Medicine (www.nlm.nih.gov/) were established, while Michael Hart's Project Gutenberg brought the rise of free access to thousands of out-of-copyright digitised texts. By the 1980s academics and researchers, especially those in science, technology, engineering and medicine, were using the pre-web internet to communicate work. By the end of the decade, several online, peer-reviewed journals had been published. However, it was a combination of the inflated costs of serials subscriptions and the arrival of the web as a new method of distribution and publication that led to the development of open access, leading to what is arguably the most significant change in scholarly communication since the invention of printing.[47]

In 1991, Paul Ginsparg founded arXiv at Los Alamos National Laboratory in the US as a solution to the problem of physicists filling up each others' e-mail boxes with documents. arXiv operated as a free, central location for scientists at the lab to share and access high-energy physics preprints. With the advent of the web in 1993, scientific researchers from around the world began depositing preprints in arXiv. This significantly improved the distribution of preprints and the timescale in which researchers could access research outputs. Previously, researchers would not have had access to research information for months or years, as papers made their way through the peer-review process before being published in academic journals. Today's institutional repositories are based on the general principles arXiv.

In the early 2000s three significant public statements were made that defined various open access concepts, outlined their principles and benefits, and helped bring the open access movement to the mainstream. In February 2002, the Budapest Open Access Initiative (BOAI; www.budapestopenaccessinitiative.org/) formally defined 'open access' for the first time, and launched a worldwide campaign to raise awareness of its benefits, encouraging individuals and institutions to sign the initiative and commit to making the outputs of their research openly available. BOAI recommended that academics and researchers self-archive their work into open repositories (known as 'green open access') and publish their papers and research in open access journals (known as 'gold open access'), thereby reaching the widest audience possible. By 2016, more than 6000 individuals and 921 organisations signed the initiative.[48]

In April 2003 the Bethesda Statement on Open Access Publishing was published. It coined the term 'open access publication' and recognised the benefits and impact of the internet on scholarly communication, demonstrating how scientists, organisations, publishers and researchers could transition to open publishing.[49] In October that same year, the directors of 19 German research organisations signed the Berlin Declaration on Open Access to Knowledge in the Sciences and Humanities. The declaration, like the Bethesda Statement, recognised and welcomed the new paradigm for academic publishing and outlined how researchers should go about making their work openly available.[50]

Advocating on behalf of the open movement

The open movement is supported by many individuals, groups, communities and organisations that advocate and lobby for openness, use and reuse of data and information. Some, such as Creative Commons, the Free Software Foundation, Berners-Lee, and the governments of Nordic countries, have been mentioned in this chapter. Other influential organisations include the Wikimedia Foundation, the not-for-profit organisation that supports and distributes funds to wiki projects and chapters such as Wikipedia and Wikimedia UK (https://wikimediafoundation.org/); Open Knowledge International (https://okfn.org/), a not-for-profit organisation that supports a network of international individuals in advocating, training and creating open knowledge and data; and the Open Data Institute (https://theodi.org/), an organisation that champions open data and works with and supports individuals, businesses, organisations and governments in their creation, curation and use of open data.

Notes

1   Historical Society of Pennsylvania, Letter from Sir Isaac Newton to Robert Hooke, 1678,
    http://digitallibrary.hsp.org/index.php/Detail/Object/Show/object_id/9285.

2   Open Definition, Open Definition 2.1, n.d., http://opendefinition.org/od/2.1/en/.

3   Butterfield, A. and Ngondi G. E. (eds), Open-Source. In *A Dictionary of Computer Science*, 7th edn, Oxford University Press, 2016,
    www.oxfordreference.com/view/10.1093/acref/9780199688975.001.0001/acref-9780199688975-e-6423.

4   AT&T BREAKUP II: highlights in the history of a telecommunications giant, *Los Angeles Times*, 21 September 1995, http://articles.latimes.com/1995-09-21/business/fi-48462_1_system-breakup.

5   Weber, S., *The Success of Open Source*, Harvard University Press, 2004, 26.

6   Open Source Initiative, The 2-Clause BSD License, n.d.,
    https://opensource.org/licenses/BSD-2-Clause.

7   Tsai, J., For Better or Worse: introducing the GNU General Public License Version 3, *Berkeley Technology Law Journal*, **23** (1), 2008, 547–81,
    www.jstor.org/stable/24118327.

8   Carver, B. W., Share and Share Alike: understanding and enforcing open source and free software licenses, *Berkeley Technology Law Journal*, 5 April 2005, papers.ssrn.com/sol3/papers.cfm?abstract_id=1586574; Williams, S., *Free as in Freedom: Richard Stallman's crusade for free software,* O'Reilly Media, 2002, Chapter 1, www.oreilly.com/openbook/freedom/ch01.html.

9   GNU, GNU General Public License, version 1, 2017,
    www.gnu.org/licenses/old-licenses/gpl-1.0.html.

10 Black Duck, Top Open Source Licenses, 2017,
    www.blackducksoftware.com/top-open-source-licenses.

11 Butterfield, A. and Ngondi G. E. (eds), World Wide Web. In *A Dictionary of Computer Science*, 7th edn, Oxford University Press, 2016,
    www.oxfordreference.com/view/10.1093/acref/9780199688975.001.0001/acref-9780199688975-e-6423.

12 Berners-Lee, T., Information Management: a proposal, 1990,
    www.dcs.gla.ac.uk/~wpc/grcs/bernerslee.pdf.

13   CERN, Ten Years Public Domain for the Original Web Software, European
      Organization for Nuclear Research, 1993,
      http://tenyears-www.web.cern.ch/tenyears-www/declaration/page1.html.

14   Boston Consulting Group, The Internet Now Contributes 10 Percent of GDP to
      the UK Economy, Surpassing the Manufacturing and Retail Sectors, press release,
      1 May 2015, www.bcg.com/d/press/1may2015-internet-contributes-10-percent-
      gdp-uk-economy-12111.

15   Crane, P. and Conaghan, J. (eds), Creative Common. In *New Oxford Companion
      to Law*, Oxford University Press, 2009,
      www.oxfordreference.com/view/10.1093/acref/9780199290543.001.0001/
      acref-9780199290543-e-515.

16   Creative Commons, State of the Commons, 2016,
      https://stateof.creativecommons.org/.

17   Hewlett Foundation, Open Educational Resources, 2016,
      www.hewlett.org/strategy/open-educational-resources/.

18   MIT OpenCourseWare, Milestone Celebration, 2017,
      https://ocw.mit.edu/about/our-history/milestone-celebration;
      Massachusetts Institute of Technology, MIT Facts 2017: mission, 2017,
      http://web.mit.edu/facts/mission.html.

19   Mellon, Hewlett Foundations Grant $11M to Launch Free MIT Course Materials
      on Web, *MIT News*, 18 June 2001, http://news.mit.edu/2001/ocwfund.

20   Khan Academy, Is Khan Academy Available In Other Languages?, n.d.,
      https://khanacademy.zendesk.com/hc/en-us/articles/202483750-Is-Khan-
      Academy-available-in-other-languages-.

21   Thomas, A., Campbell, L. M., Barker, P. and Hawksey, M. (eds), *Into the Wild:
      technology for open educational resources*, 2012, http://publications.cetis.org.uk/
      wp-content/uploads/2012/12/into_the_wild_screen.pdf.

22   Green, C., Open Licensing and Open Education Licensing Policy. In Jhangiani,
      R. S. and Biswas-Diener, R. (eds), *Open: the philosophy and practices that are
      revolutionizing education and science*, Ubiquity Press, 2017, 29–41,
      www.ubiquitypress.com/site/chapters/10.5334/bbc.c/download/591/.

23   Scassa, T., Privacy and Open Government, *Future Internet*, **6** (2), 397–413, 2014,
      www.mdpi.com/1999-5903/6/2/397.

24   Wolf, P., The 50th Anniversary of the Freedom of Information Act?, 23 June 2016,
      http://artvoice.com/2016/06/23/50th-anniversary-freedom-information-act/.

25   National Archives, *Guide to House Records*, 2016, Chapter 11,
      www.archives.gov/legislative/guide/house/chapter-11-government-
      operations.html.

26 Blanton, T. and Harper, L. (eds), FOIA@50, National Security Archive, 1 July 2016, http://nsarchive.gwu.edu/NSAEBB/NSAEBB554-FOIA@50/.

27 Government Offices of Sweden, The Swedish Press Act: 250 years of freedom of the press, 2 June 2016, www.government.se/articles/2016/06/the-swedish-press-act-250-years-of-freedom-of-the-press2/.

28 Ginsberg, W., The Freedom of Information Act (FOIA): background, legislation, and policy issues, Congressional Research Service, 2014, https://fas.org/sgp/crs/secrecy/R41933.pdf; Electronic Frontier Foundation, History of FOIA, 2016, www.eff.org/issues/transparency/history-of-foia.

29 Gomes, Á. and Soares, D., Open Government Data Initiatives in Europe: northern versus southern countries analysis. In *Proceedings of the 8th International Conference on Theory and Practice of Electronic Governance* 27 October 2014, 342–50.

30 National Archives, History of the Public Records Acts, n.d., www.nationalarchives.gov.uk/information-management/legislation/public-records-act/history-of-pra/; Carr, V., The Public Record Office, The National Archives and the historian, Making History, 2008, www.history.ac.uk/makinghistory/resources/articles/PRO_TNA.html.

31 Gov.UK, Your right to know: the Governments proposals for a Freedom of Information Act, Cabinet Office, 1997, www.gov.uk/government/publications/your-right-to-know-the-governments-proposals-for-a-freedom-of-information-act.

32 See Free Our Data, Make Taxpayers' Data Available To Them, n.d., www.freeourdata.org.uk/; Free Our Data, *Guardian*, 2017, www.theguardian.com/technology/free-our-data.

33 Office of Fair Trading, Commercial use of public information, 2006, http://webarchive.nationalarchives.gov.uk/20140402142426/http:/www.oft.gov.uk/OFTwork/markets-work/public-information.

34 Cross, M., Data Restrictions Cost Economy £500m, *Guardian*, 14 December 2006, https://www.theguardian.com/technology/2006/dec/14/freeourdata.epublic.

35 Arthur, C., 'OK, Let's Do It': How Britain's official data was freed, *Guardian*, 21 January 2010, www.theguardian.com/technology/2010/jan/21/how-official-data-freed.

36 Grønbech-Jensen, C., The Scandinavian Tradition of Open Government and the European Union: problems of compatibility?, *Journal of European Public Policy*, 4 February 2011, www.tandfonline.com/doi/abs/10.1080/13501768880000091; Centre Virtuel de la Connaissance sur l'Europe, Treaty on European Union — Declaration No 17 on the right of access to information, 7 February 1992,

www.cvce.eu/content/publication/2006/10/25/c93fe321-0e77-43a0-b316-
d0d45635ff98/publishable_en.pdf; Harlow, C. and Rawlings, R., *Process and
Procedure in EU Administration*, Hart, 2014.

37   Tauberer, J., Open Government Data Definition: the 8 principles of open
government data. In *Open Government Data: the book*, 2nd edn, 2014,
https://opengovdata.io/2014/8-principles/.

38   White House Archives, Transparency and Open Government, memorandum, 21
January 2009, https://obamawhitehouse.archives.gov/the-press-office/
transparency-and-open-government; Executive Office of the President,
Memorandum for the Heads of Executive Departments and Agencies,
8 November 2016,
https://obamawhitehouse.archives.gov/sites/default/files/omb/memoranda/
2017/m-17-06.pdf.

39   Open Government Partnership, What is the Open Government Partnership?,
2015, www.opengovpartnership.org/.

40   Open Data Handbook, Open Data, n.d.,
http://opendatahandbook.org/glossary/en/terms/open-data/.

41   National Academies of Science, Engineering and Medicine, Summary. In *Earth
Observations from Space: the first 50 years of scientific achievements*, National
Academies Press, 2008, www.nap.edu/read/11991/chapter/2; Chignard, S., A Brief
History of Open Data, *Paris Innovation Review*, 29 March 2013,
www.paristechreview.com/2013/03/29/brief-history-open-data/; ICSU World Data
System, About, n.d., www.icsu-wds.org/organization.

42   CERN, Computing, European Organization for Nuclear Research, 2017,
https://home.cern/about/computing; Datasets – Data.gov.uk,
https://data.gov.uk/data/search?q=census.

43   Berners-Lee, T., Hendler, J. and Lassila, O., The Semantic Web: web content that
is meaningful to computers will unleash a revolution of new possibilities, *Scientific
American*, May 2001, https://www-
sop.inria.fr/acacia/cours/essi2006/Scientific%20American_%20Feature%20Article_
%20The%20Semantic%20Web_%20May%202001.pdf.

44   Last, M., 5 Star Open Data, 2015, http://5stardata.info/.

45   Budapest Open Access Initiative, BOAI 15, 2002,
www.budapestopenaccessinitiative.org/boai15-1.

46   Education Resources Information Center, 50 Years of ERIC: 1964–2014, 2014,
https://eric.ed.gov/pdf/ERIC_Retrospective.pdf.

47   Suber, P., Timeline of the Open Access Movement, 2009,
http://legacy.earlham.edu/~peters/fos/timeline.htm.

48 Budapest Open Access Initiative, BOAI 15, 2002,
    www.budapestopenaccessinitiative.org/boai15-1.

49 Earlham College, Bethesda Statement on Open Access Publishing, 20 June 2003,
    http://legacy.earlham.edu/~peters/fos/bethesda.htm.

50 Max Planck Open Access, Berlin Declaration on Open Access to Knowledge in
    the Sciences and Humanities, 22 October 2003,
    https://openaccess.mpg.de/67605/berlin_declaration_engl.pdf.

Chapter 3

Copyright and licensing: a background

Introduction

This chapter provides an overview of copyright and other intellectual property rights, giving background and context to the development of intellectual property licensing, openness and the open movement. After describing rights such as those afforded by patents and trademarks, the chapter focuses on copyright and how original creative works are intellectually protected in the UK, Europe and internationally. A key section of the chapter addresses the 'threshold of originality', which can be of critical importance to cultural organisations engaged in digitisation work. Finally, the chapter describes the components and purposes of licensing and open licences and gives context to the concept of the public domain and the expiration of copyright.

Intellectual property rights

Licensing, openness and the open movement outlined in the preceding chapter partly arise as a reaction to the presence of intellectual property rights. These are a collection of associated property rights, which each afford protection to a particular aspect of intellectual creation. In the UK there are five intellectual property rights: patents, trademarks, registered designs, design right and copyright.[1] The first three of these rights are registered rights. Such rights do not arise naturally, and only afford protection following a successful application and registration process. The latter two rights, design right and copyright, are automatic rights, which arise naturally and do not need to be registered.

Patents

Patents provide protection for inventions and innovations. There is a particularly long tradition of patenting in the UK, with the first recorded English patent being granted in 1449.[2] This grant provided John of Utynam, who had devised a novel glass-producing technique, a 20-year monopoly on the right to exploit his invention in England. Because the purpose of a patent is to grant a monopoly exploitation right to an inventor of something new, which has advanced the current state-of-the-art, registration places a heavy emphasis on the demonstration of innovation and applicability.

Today patent registration authorities, such as the UK Intellectual Property Office, publish patent applications and grants online. This makes patenting something of a dichotomous activity. On the one hand, seeking a patent exposes an invention in minute detail. On the other hand, once registered, for a period of time, the patent holder enjoys the sole right to benefit from that invention. An inventor retains the option to keep their novelty secret and not seek a patent. However, such an approach comes with the risk that, if exposed when unregistered, such an invention could be copied and replicated by others, to the inventor's disadvantage.

Innovators do not always view protection and monopolisation of the state-of-the-art as the most advantageous position. A recent move towards openness has emerged in the patent sphere, notably among major innovating firms, such as Tesla and IBM.[3] Announcing in 2014 its decision for 'applying the open source philosophy' to its patents, electric carmaker Tesla explained that it was initially 'compelled' to protect its inventions through patenting out of 'concern' that larger, more established competitors would quickly capitalise on the new state-of-the-art and outpace it in production and sales. Tesla described its shift towards openness as being founded on a reverse theory to the closed patent concept, whereby 'the world would all benefit from a common, rapidly-evolving technology platform', which could not be built in the short term without other carmakers being able to exploit and build on the state-of-the-art that Tesla had devised.[4]

Trademarks

Trademarks provide brand protection for names and logos associated with goods and services. On 1 January 1876 Bass Ale obtained the first registered trademark protection in the UK. This registration is still in place as trademark UK00000000001 and is next due for renewal by the current owners in 2022.[5] In the UK, trademarks can consist of words, sounds, logos, colours, or a combination of these.[6] Trademarks are distinctive indicators of particular goods and services. Trademark UK00000000001, for example, provides protection for the labelling of a particular brand of pale ale. Through registration, other pale ales cannot use a markedly similar label, which in turn allows Bass to remain distinctive. Through additional trademarks the owners of trademark UK00000000001 are also able, for example, to protect the word 'Bass', in relation to the sale of ale, the distinctive red triangle logo of the beer, and other identifiers used to market the product.

Trademarks are registered by category. In the example of trademark UK00000000001, the mark is protected in just one category: class 32 (Beers; Mineral and aerated waters and other non-alcoholic beverages; Fruit beverages and fruit juices; syrups and other preparations for making beverages), specifically 'pale ale'. Registration by class means that trademarks do not necessarily relate to a full range of goods and services. In part, this enables brands with similar or the same design, branding or name to operate in their respective areas without conflict. When established businesses venture into new fields, however, classification can prove problematic. For example, the Apple technology firm's move into the music sales business (opening the iTunes store and selling iPod MP3 players) caused a trademark dispute with the established record label Apple.[7]

In the UK there are currently 45 trademark classes. Classes 1–34 are for certification of goods and classes 35–45 are for certification of services. At registration, applicants are asked to select the class or classes in which they wish to protect their mark. The more classes that a mark is registered in, the higher the cost of registration. If a business is likely only to sell goods or services in one or two classes, it may be in their interests only to make a limited registration. For example, a firm seeking to protect a logo used to sell coffee may only need protection in the UK under class 30. However, if hoping to market a range of beverages in the UK, the same company may wish to widen its trademark application to also include class 29 (Milk and milk products) and class 32 (Mineral and aerated waters and other non-alcoholic beverages; Fruit beverages and fruit juices).

The UK Intellectual Property Office registers trademarks and currently advises that applications take around four months to process. Once registered, trademarks last for ten years and can then be renewed.

There is no particular 'open trademark' tradition. There is no requirement to register a trademark in order to use a name, logo, sound or colour. However, the risks associated with marketing goods and services under a name or logo without registration is that a competitor could usurp an established position by registering the mark.

As visual or auditory works, trademarks can crucially also be subject to other intellectual property rights: such as copyright and design right.

Registered designs

A registered design protects the look of a product. In the UK, a registered design can protect, in particular, the appearance, shape, configuration, or decoration of a product.[8] Unlike a patent, a protected design specifically protects elements of an item that are structured for design purposes, not for innovative functional purposes.

This right should not be confused with a trademark, which protects the application of a name or logo, nor should it be confused with a patent, which protects an invention. The right of a registered design should also not be confused with design right, which is an automatic (unregistered) right that more generally protects the shapes of objects.

For example, UK registered design 4011900 provides protection for the design of a 'part of a vacuum cleaner' and is owned by Dyson Technology Limited.[9] The design is registered by class, in this case the design is protected under subclass 05 (Washing, cleaning and drying machines) of class 15 (Machines, not elsewhere specified). Unlike a patent, this registered design protects the look of the vacuum cleaner part, not any innovative functional aspect of the machine.

Design right

Design right is one of the two primary automatic intellectual property rights in the UK, the other being copyright (along with its related rights). Design right should not be confused with registered design right, which is not an automatic right. Design right specifically protects the 'shape and configuration' of objects: 'how different parts of a design are arranged together'.[10]

Because design right is an automatic right, there is no formal registration process as with patents, trademarks or registered designs. The protection afforded by design right arises automatically and remains in place either for a fixed period of ten years from when the design was first sold or 15 years from when the design was first made, whichever period is shorter.

Copyright

Copyright is an automatic, unregistered right that protects original, recorded creations of the mind. Like design right, there is no requirement in the UK to register a work in order to receive copyright protection. Indeed, there is no registration mechanism.

As with other intellectual property rights, copyright is time limited. In general, copyright reserves certain rights to the owner, including the right to make copies of the work, the right to make adaptations of the work, the right to communicate the work to the public, and the right to distribute copies of the work to the public.

The modern, international copyright system has its roots in the UK's 18th-century publishing laws and a series of increasingly expansive international agreements established from the mid-19th century onwards.

Today's tradition of statutory copyright protection for authors originated with the UK's Statute of Anne in 1710.[11] Before 1710, the Livery Company of printers and publishers, commonly referred to as the Stationers Company, enjoyed monopoly printing rights under the terms of the Licensing of the Press Act 1662.[12] Under this system only members of the Company could publish works. As a result, the flow of printed information from the comparatively cheap printing press technology was heavily controlled, centralised and regulated.

The Statute of Anne, conversely, handed monopoly rights to the authors of written works, not to a single trade guild or to publishers or printers. The statute gave authors the exclusive right to control the printing and publication of their own written works for a defined (normally 14-year) term. Only the author, and the printers they chose to license, could print a text. The term of exclusive control could be extended for one further 14-year term, if the author was still alive at the end of the first term. Once the right expired, however, the work entered the public domain and any printer was able to publish it without legal restriction.

Although long-replaced by subsequent copyright systems and regulations, the Statute of Anne represents a shift in the concept of protection for written works. The statute's protection for authors, as opposed to printers, marks a turning point and has had direct influence on today's copyright protections.

Copyright in the UK

The UK's primary copyright legislation, in place since 1 August 1989, is the Copyright, Designs and Patents Act 1988 (CDPA).

Types of works protected

Literary, dramatic, musical and artistic works receive copyright protection in the UK, as do sound recordings, films, broadcasts and typographical arrangements of published editions. To be protected, a work must fall within at least one of these categories, must be recorded (in some form, whether on paper, tape, digital media or otherwise), and must be original (see section 'Threshold of originality', page 37). It is important to understand what type of work something is in the eyes of copyright, as in various respects this determines the duration of protection and which copyright exceptions may or may not be relied on.

Literary works

A 'literary' work is 'any work, other than a dramatic or musical work, which is written, spoken or sung' (CDPA, s 3(1)). The written portions of a book, article, newspaper, journal, letter, e-mail or website or the lyrics of a song, by way of examples, may be protected as literary works.

Computer programs, databases and other tables or compilations are also protected as literary works. For the purposes of copyright protection, a 'database' is more widely defined than may otherwise be customary. A database is 'a collection of independent works, data or other materials' arranged in a 'systematic or methodical way' and 'individually accessible by electronic or other means' (CDPA, s 3A). To be eligible for protection, a database's selection or arrangement must be original (see section 'Threshold of originality', page 37).

Dramatic works

A 'dramatic' work is the writing, notation or other encoding of a piece intended to be performed, for example, the script of a play or the notation for a dance.

Musical works

A 'musical' work is a work of music, other than any words or lyrics, which are protected separately as a literary work. This is in reference to the music itself, rather than to any recording of the music (see section 'Sound recordings', below).

Artistic works

An 'artistic' work is any two-dimensional or three-dimensional artwork, such as a painting, photograph, etching or sculpture. Drawings, maps, plans, charts and diagrams are all classified by the CDPA as 'graphic' works and protected as artistic works. Works of artistic craftsmanship and works of architecture, including buildings and models of buildings, are similarly protected as artistic works.

Sound recordings

A 'sound recording' is any recording of sound. Other copyright-protected works may be incorporated in a sound recording. For example, a recording of a song may contain three separate types of copyright work: a musical work (in the music), a literary work (in the lyrics), and a sound recording.

Films

A 'film' is any recording of moving images, as well as any soundtrack incorporated with the moving images. A soundtrack that exists separately as a sound recording (without moving images, for example the CD of a film soundtrack) may be separately protected as a sound recording. As with sound recordings, films are particularly liable to contain numerous layers of copyright from different types of copyright works that have been incorporated in the film. A film's script, for example, is protected as a dramatic work; any lyrics in the soundtrack are protected as a literary work, and so on.

Broadcasts

A 'broadcast' is an electronic transmission of image, sound or other information transmitted for simultaneous reception by the public or at a time specifically determined by the transmitter for public reception.

Published editions

The typographical arrangement of a published edition of 'the whole or any part of one or more literary, dramatic or musical works' is also subject to copyright protection (CDPA, s. 8). A published edition that reproduces the typographical arrangement of a previous edition is not eligible for fresh protection.

As noted, a single material item can contain multiple types of copyright work. For example, a book may contain both 'literary' and 'artistic' material. A sound recording may contain literary work (in the lyrics) and musical work (in the tune), as well as attracting overall protection as a recording.

Threshold of originality

As an unregistered right, copyright arises simply when a qualifying work is recorded. Whereas an innovation is not protected by a patent until the validity of protection has been argued for and proactively handed out by an authority, unregistered intellectual property rights simply come into being. There are broadly three elements that determine whether a work qualifies for copyright protection: the authorship and creation of the work, the recording of the work, and the originality of the work.

The first of these elements, authorship and creation, while important, has a lesser significance today than it may previously have had (see section 'Copyright around the world', page 46). The location of a work's creation, where a work is first published, and where an author is based all impact on its qualification for copyright protection. However, as a result of international agreements in place today it can broadly be assumed that a work qualifies for protection in the UK.

The second element of qualification is the need to be in a recorded form. This is the simplest test of qualification. Copyright does not protect ideas or otherwise that have not been recorded. For example, literary works historically tended to be recorded on paper or parchment, but copyright places no restriction on the method of recording. Under the recording test a literary work qualifies as much for protection when digitally encoded as binary 1s and 0s, or indeed when sprayed onto a wall, as it does when typeset into a paper book.

The third of these qualification tests concerns the originality of a work, and is significantly more challenging to unpick. Under section 1 of the CDPA, only 'original' literary, dramatic, musical and artistic works qualify for protection (CDPA, s. 1). Historically, in order to determine whether a work may be considered 'original', English law has focused on the effort that has gone into 'originating' (or creating) it. This is known as the 'sweat of the brow' doctrine.

Although determined under the Copyright Act 1842, *Walter* v *Lane* (1900) remains the pivotal case in respect of this doctrine.[13] A speech delivered by Lord Rosebery was noted down in shorthand by journalists. One journalist published the speech in *The Times*, and claimed a copyright in that publication of the work. In *Walter* v *Lane* the House of Lords considered whether the journalist's noting, rewriting and publication of the speech was sufficiently 'original' to warrant copyright protection. The Lords found in favour and upheld that copyright did subsist in the published account, distinguishing between the work that Lord Rosebery created (the speech) and the work that the journalist created (the noted, edited and re-transcribed account of the speech) as two distinct works. The effort that the journalist placed into creating the second work ensured that, to the Lords, there was sufficient originality for a fresh copyright protection. This was so even though the aims of the journalist were to report on and reflect the speech accurately. Therefore the sweat of the brow doctrine sets a determinedly low threshold of originality.

In contrast to the British tradition of sweat of the brow, European copyright regulation and interpretation has centred on the concept of an 'author's intellectual creation'. A pivotal case was the 2009 Infopaq decision of the Court of Justice of the European Union, the highest judicial authority of the EU (see section 'The European Union', page 48). In its decision, the Court concluded that the 'intellectual creation' threshold, which is explicitly applicable under EU regulations to certain types of works, such as computer programs, extends also to all copyright works of authorship as defined in the InfoSoc Directive (Council Directive 2001/29/EC). The phrase 'author's own intellectual creation' does not appear in that directive. However, the Court, citing the harmonisation aspirations of the directive, determined that copyright for authored works of any type 'is liable to apply only in relation to a subject-matter which is original in the sense that it is its author's own intellectual creation'.[14]

The copyright laws of some EU member states draw more directly on this threshold than the UK's 1988 Act. For example, copyright in France protects works that are *une création intellectuelle originale* ('an original intellectual creation') and French law specifies that to qualify for protection a work must be *œuvres de l'esprit* ('works of the mind').[15] German copyright law specifically provides protection to works that are *geistige Schöpfungen* ('intellectual creations').[16]

The gulf between what qualifies as a copyright work under the sweat of the brow tradition and what qualifies for protection under the doctrine of authorial intellectual creation can become significant, particularly in relation to faithful reproductions of other works, whether transcribed speeches (as in the case of *Walter* v *Lane*) or digitised surrogates of other works (as is rapidly becoming business as usual activity for cultural heritage organisations). Under the doctrine of authorial intellectual creation, a pertinent question becomes whether the creation of a copy in the digitisation process includes any elements of intellectual creation by the author of the new work (e.g. the digitisation operative). If not, under this doctrine, as set out by the Court of Justice, such works do not qualify for copyright protection.

There remains uncertainty as to whether faithful two-dimensional reproductions of other works qualify for copyright protection. The UK's Intellectual Property Office cited this ongoing uncertainty in a non-legal notice issued in November 2015, which was a rare public attempt by an intellectual property authority to tackle the question of digitisation of public domain works head on. Although largely just a short observation of the uncertainty, the notice highlights that the Court of Justice decision in the Infopaq case concluded that authorial intellectual creation is the relevant threshold and that (at the time of the judgment as well as of writing) Court of Justice decisions are binding in the UK as elsewhere in the EU. The Intellectual Property Office's Copyright Notice states:

Given this criteria, it seems unlikely that what is merely a retouched, digitised image of an older work can be considered as 'original'. This is because there will generally be minimal scope for a creator to exercise free and creative choices if their aim is simply to make a faithful reproduction of an existing work.[17]

Copyright ownership

The first owner of copyright in a work is normally the author. If there are multiple authors of a work, whose contributions are indistinguishable from one another's (like this chapter of this book), the work is of joint authorship and all authors are jointly the first owners of copyright. Copyright in a work created in the course of employment is normally first owned by the employer, not the employee(s) who author the work, unless there is a contract term that states otherwise.

As a property right, copyright ownership can be transferred (see section 'Assignation', page 48). The first owner of copyright in many cases may not remain the owner for the duration of the protection. For example, where a literary work is not created during employment, the author is the first owner of the copyright. Protection in a literary work of known authorship lasts for 70 years after the death of the last living author. By definition, therefore, even if the author does not transfer or assign their rights within their lifetime, unless the rights are waived, the copyright is ultimately owned by at least one other party.

Crown copyright

A work created by the monarch, or by a servant of the monarch in the course of their duties, is protected in the UK by Crown copyright. In most respects, Crown copyright is identical to standard copyright protection. The key difference is duration, with Crown works normally being protected for shorter periods than comparable non-Crown works. Works created by government departments and acts of parliament are protected by Crown copyright. Crown copyright works have a notable presence in the sphere of open licensing, being some of the works most likely to be openly licensed and easily reusable (see section 'The Open Government Licence', page 57).

Acts restricted by copyright

The owner of a copyright retains the exclusive right to control the six acts restricted by copyright in relation to that work, for the duration of the term of protection. The six acts restricted by copyright are listed in section 16 of the CDPA:

- the right to copy the work
- the right to issue copies of the work to the public
- the right to rent or lend the work to the public
- the right to perform, show, or play the work in public
- the right to communicate the work to the public
- the right to make an adaptation of the work or to do any of the above in relation to making an adaptation.

These are collectively the 'economic' rights. Further rights, known as 'moral' rights are subject to different rules and are explored in the section 'Moral rights', page 42.

It is the property ownership prerogative of a rights owner to determine how, whether and to what extent they wish to use or share the exercise of these rights. Intentionally or otherwise, a copyright owner may opt never to exercise any rights or to allow others to exercise those rights in any manner. For example, the author of a diary may never undertake any of these acts. The author of a novel or the illustrator of a children's TV series, on the other hand, may undertake extensive use of the restricted acts, as a necessary element of ensuring the creation is seen and enjoyed by others.

When copyright protection lapses (see section 'The public domain', page 60) the right to control the undertaking of these acts ceases and no person or persons may monopolise these rights. During the lifetime of the copyright, only the owner, or a person to whom the owner or a person acting with the authority of the owner has given permission, may undertake the restricted acts in relation to the work. The granting of permission by the copyright owner to others in this manner is undertaken through licensing.

Additionally and fundamentally the exclusive rights provided by copyright are countered by statutory exceptions, known as exceptions to copyright (see section 'Exceptions and limitations', page 44). These exceptions enable certain and limited types of use without the need for permission from the copyright owner.

It is important to stress that the right to exclusive control of the restricted acts is afforded to the copyright owner, not necessarily to the author(s) of a work. If the author of a work is not the copyright owner, for example because the work was created in the course of employment or the ownership was transferred, then the author requires the owner's permission to undertake the economic acts restricted by copyright or needs to rely on an exception, just as any other non-owner.

Moral rights

In addition to the six economic rights provided through copyright protection, authors of intellectual works benefit from four moral rights in the UK:

- the right to be identified as the author of a work
- the right to object to derogatory treatment of a work
- the right not to be falsely attributed as the author of a work
- the right to privacy in relation to photographs and films commissioned for private purposes.

Unlike economic rights, moral rights may not be licensed or assigned. However, moral rights can be waived. Moral rights only derive in relation to literary, dramatic, musical and artistic works, as well as films and certain performances.

Duration

Like other intellectual property rights, copyright is time limited. Since the Statute of Anne, when a work could be protected for a maximum of 28 years, duration has increased significantly. Duration is normally associated with the lifetime of the author or authors, not the date of creation. However, if the copyright owner is not the author, duration is not associated with the lifespan of the copyright owner, it continues to be associated with the lifespan of the author(s).

'Standard' copyright duration for literary, dramatic, musical and artistic works in the UK is for a period of 70 years after the end of the year in which the last living author or creator died. The standard term for films is also a period of 70 years after the end of the year in which the last living principal director, screenplay author, dialogue author or composer of music specifically created for the film died. The standard term for sound recordings is 50 years from the end of the year in which the recording was made or, if made available to the public in that time, 50 years from the end of the year on which it was first made available.

When the 1988 Act first came into force, 'standard' copyright duration for literary, dramatic, musical and artistic works was for a period of 50 years from the end of the year in which the last author died. The 20-year extension to raise this period to 70 years came into force from 1 January 1996 by virtue of the Duration of Copyright and Rights in Performances Regulations 1995. The 1995

Regulations transposed into UK law the terms of Council Directive 93/98/EEC of the European Council, which harmonised certain elements of copyright duration in Europe. Any works that were still protected by copyright in the UK when the regulations came into force benefited from the extension. Significantly, works that had entered the public domain in the UK had their rights revived in some cases. Any work that would have benefited from copyright protection elsewhere in the European Economic Area (EEA) on 1 July 1995 had copyright revived under the 1995 Regulations. Copyright in a published literary work by an author who died in 1940, for example, would have expired at the end of 1990 under the 1988 Act as first enacted. However, because copyright protection was afforded for published literary works for a period of 70 years after the death of the author in certain EEA jurisdictions (notably Germany), copyright would have been revived on 1 January 1996 and expired again at the end of 2010 (because had the work been created in some other part of the EEA, like Germany, it would still have been protected on 1 July 1995).

There are many factors that can impact on copyright duration and many works are subject to a period of protection that differs from the standard term. Whether a work has a known author and whether a work has been published are two factors that most significantly determine copyright duration.

The vagaries of copyright duration are particularly acute in the UK in relation to unpublished literary, dramatic, musical and artistic works. Any such work that was unpublished on 1 August 1989 (the day the current copyright act, the CDPA, came into force) and had at least one author who died before 1 January 1969 is protected by copyright until the end of 31 December 2039, irrespective of how long it has been since the last author died. Unpublished works with authors who all died from 1 January 1969 onwards receive 'standard' copyright protection, which protects them beyond the end of 2039. This quirk of duration can have a significant impact on archival collections held in the UK, which primarily comprise unpublished older works that fall within this '2039 duration'.

It is a moot point when determining copyright duration, and therefore copyright subsistence, whether any or all copyright owners can be identified or located. The fact that an owner cannot be found or is not taking positive action to assert their rights does not mean that the protection is void. A work that is protected by copyright and where one or more of the copyright owners are unknown or cannot be located is known as an 'orphan work'. Orphan works are in-copyright works and under law need to continue to be treated as such. In the EU and the UK there are now mechanisms for enabling greater use of orphan works – although these are limited in scope.

Exceptions and limitations

Copyright law provides for certain exceptions and limitations to the otherwise exclusive economic rights enjoyed by copyright owners. In principle, exceptions and limitations stipulate 'cases in which protected works may be used without the authorisation of the rightholder and with or without payment of compensation'.[18]

The specific exceptions and limitations available to users of copyright material vary between countries, although these are largely underpinned by supra-state (in the case of the EU) and international baseline standards. The primary underpinning standard is the so-called 'three-step test', which derives from the Berne Convention and details the fundamental criteria by which any exception or limitation to economic rights in Berne signatory states must comply (see section 'The Berne Convention', page 46).

The EU Directive on harmonisation of certain aspects of copyright and related rights in the information society (the InfoSoc Directive; see section 'The European Union', page 48) was developed in order to advance a 'harmonised legal framework on copyright and related rights' (Council Directive 2001/29/EC, Recital 4) and to transpose the World Intellectual Property Organization (WIPO) Copyright Treaty and WIPO Performances and Phonograms Treaty (see section 'WIPO', page 47) into EU regulations. A particular feature of the InfoSoc Directive was the provision of an 'exhaustive enumeration of exceptions and limitations to the reproduction right and the right of communication to the public' (Council Directive 2001/29/EC, Recital 32). The directive stipulated: 'Member States should arrive at a coherent application of these exceptions and limitations' (Council Directive 2001/29/EC, Recital 32).

Accordingly, certain exceptions and limitations have been delineated in UK law. These are primarily set out in Chapter III of the Copyright, Designs and Patents Act 1988 (CDPA). A number of the UK copyright exceptions are premised on requiring that the beneficiary of the exception is able to make a defence of 'fair dealing'. In effect fair dealing acts as a qualification on these exceptions. In order for their use to be legal, a beneficiary must comply with a specific copyright exception (see summaries below) and, in the case of a fair dealing exception, ensure that their use of material in accordance with that purpose can be defended as 'fair'. Copyright legislation does not provide a definition of what constitutes 'fair dealing' or fairness in this respect. Instead, the parameters of what constitutes fair dealing have been developed by interpretation, guidance and the courts. A key interpretation comes from *Hyde Park Residences* v *Yelland* (2000). The Hyde Park judgment concluded that in assessing whether a use was defensible under the premise of fair dealing, the Court had to 'judge the fairness by the objective standard of whether a fair minded and honest person would have dealt with the copyright work' in the same manner.[19]

More practical interpretation can focus on the specific amounts of a work that may be copied and reused fairly under a relevant exception. For example, the Bodleian Library at the University of Oxford provides a short list of the 'generally accepted upper limits of what constitutes a substantial amount that can be copied within "fair dealing"', which includes, for example, 'one complete chapter from a book' and 'one case report from a law report'.[20] Although such 'best estimate' upper limits can be useful, it is worth bearing in mind that 'fairness' is not only a consideration of an amount, and that any best guidance amounts are not set in stone and may be subject to variance based on other relevant factors (including whether the work is published, the purpose and the nature of the reuser). Latest advice from the Chartered Institute of Library and Information Professionals (CILIP) and the Libraries and Archives Copyright Alliance outlines that 'fair' amounts in most cases 'should be judged on a case by case basis' and notes that '5% of a published work could possibly be reasonable' in certain situations.[21]

The UK copyright exceptions are likely to be of most direct relevance to the work of cultural heritage organisations and users. The general exceptions are:

- research and private study (s. 29)
- text and data mining (s. 29a)
- criticism and review (s. 30)
- quotation (s. 30)
- news reporting (s. 30)
- caricature, parody or pastiche (s. 30a)
- incidental inclusion (s. 31)
- copies of works for disabled persons (ss. 31A–31F).

The education exception is:

- illustration for instruction (s. 32).

The libraries and archives exceptions are:

- lending of copies (s. 40a)
- making works available through dedicated terminals (s. 40b)
- supplying copies to other libraries (s. 41)

- replacement copies (s. 42)
- single copies of published works (s. 42a)
- single copies of unpublished works (s. 43)
- certain permitted uses of orphan works (s. 44b, s. 76a and Schedule ZA1)
- parliamentary and judicial proceedings, royal commissions and statutory inquiries (ss. 45–6).

There are various further exceptions and limitations concerned, among other things, with public records, computer programs, databases, designs, typefaces, anonymous and pseudonymous works, public readings and recitations, article abstracts, recording of folksongs, publicly situated buildings and sculptures, lending, incidental recording for broadcasts, recording broadcasts for time-shifting, public showing of broadcasts, and recording of broadcasts for archival purposes.

A number of copyright exceptions were revised or introduced into UK regulations in 2014, following recommendations set out by the report *Digital Opportunity* in 2011 (the so-called 'Hargreaves Review').[22] As well as introducing new exceptions into UK law (derived from EU law, and in particular the list of permissible exceptions set out in the InfoSoc Directive; see section 'The European Union', page 48), the 2014 changes improved the structure of existing exceptions. In particular, many exceptions that were limited to specific types of copyright work (e.g. literary, dramatic and artistic works) were reworded to cover simply 'works' or 'items'. Several exceptions also now benefit from a ban on contract override, so a legal agreement cannot introduce any term that would prevent the lawful exercise of a relevant copyright exception (e.g. fair dealing with a work for non-commercial research or private study) and any such terms are void in so far as they prohibit a person from benefiting from a relevant copyright exception.

Copyright around the world

The Berne Convention

The Berne Convention, first adopted in 1886 and most recently revised in 1971, sets out several key international principles of modern copyright protection. In particular it

- provides for mutual protection for works in any Berne Convention signatory country authored by a national of another such country – for example, a South African author's work receives the same copyright protection in Germany that a German author's work would receive

● provides for the right of automatic protection without the need to register – this contrasts with the preceding practice in various jurisdictions, such as the UK, where protection was premised on registration

● provides a minimum period of protection for 50 years after the year in which an author dies

● establishes the standardised basis for certain exceptions and limitations to the otherwise exclusive rights afforded by copyright – this is done in particular through the so-called 'three-step test', which exceptions must comply with; Article 9(2) of the Convention sets out the test by allowing signatory states 'to permit the reproduction of such works in [1] *certain special cases*, provided that such reproduction [2] *does not conflict with a normal exploitation of the work* and [3] *does not unreasonably prejudice the legitimate interests of the author*' (numbering and emphasis added to indicate the so-called three steps).[23]

A significant majority of states are signatory to the Berne Convention, which currently has 173 contracting parties.[24] The UK signed the Convention in 1886 and ratified its signature in 1887. The US, by contrast, did not accede to the Convention for another century, finally doing so in 1988.

WIPO

The World Intellectual Property Organization (WIPO) is an agency of the United Nations with responsibility for co-ordinating intellectual property services, policy, information and co-operation across 188 member states.[25] WIPO was founded in 1967 and is based in Geneva, Switzerland. The organisation administers various international intellectual property schemes, such as the Madrid system for international trademark registration and the Hague system for international design registration. WIPO's Standing Committee on Copyright and Related Rights has since 1998 acted as a major international forum for the development of copyright regulation. WIPO administers various international copyright treaties, including the Berne Convention.

The WIPO Copyright Treaty was agreed in 1996 and entered into force in the EU and UK in 2010. The Treaty was incorporated into EU law by the InfoSoc Directive (see section 'The European Union', page 48) in 2001. The Treaty is concerned with advancing for the digital area the protection standards set out in the Berne Convention and deals with the protection of computer programs and databases and arrangements against the circumvention of technological protection measures.

TRIPS

The Agreement on Trade-Related Aspects of Intellectual Property (TRIPS) is an international agreement of the World Trade Organization that came into force on 1 January 1995. TRIPS has three primary areas of focus: standards, enforcement and dispute settlement. A key copyright function of TRIPS is the requirement to comply with the Berne Convention (with the exclusion of matters of moral rights). Other requirements of the Berne Convention are 'incorporated by reference and thus become obligations under the TRIPS Agreement between TRIPS Member countries'.[26]

TRIPS is a 'Berne plus' agreement: it largely adopts by reference the terms of the Berne Convention and adds further requirements where the Convention was found lacking or insufficient. In particular, TRIPS:

● stipulates that computer programs should be protected as literary works (Article 10.1)
● provides for databases to be protected by copyright even where the data themselves do not qualify for protection, by virtue of the selection or arrangement of the data (Article 10.2)
● provides that in the majority of cases, where duration of copyright is not calculated in relation to the lifespan of a person, such duration should be for a minimum term of 50 years from first publication or 50 years from first creation if the work remains unpublished (Article 12).

The European Union

Copyright law within the EU has to an extent been harmonised, although not to the degree of other intellectual property regimes (such as trademarks and patents). As a supranational union, unlike the World Trade Organization or the United Nations, the EU generates laws that member states are directly bound by (regulations) or are compelled to transpose into their own legislative framework (directives). Furthermore, the EU has judicial powers by means of the Court of Justice of the European Union, which is the EU's ultimate court and has responsibility for interpreting EU law. Accordingly, as well as regulating, the EU develops a corpus of copyright case law. Decisions of the Court of Justice of the European Union are binding on member states.

The primary EU law on copyright is the tediously named 'Directive 2001/29/EC of the European Parliament and of the Council of 22 May 2001 on the harmonisation of certain aspects of copyright and related rights in the information society', often known as the Information Society Directive, InfoSoc Directive or Copyright Directive. The directive implemented the WIPO Copyright Treaty and the WIPO Performances and Phonograms Treaty into European law (see preceding sections 'Exceptions and limitations' and 'WIPO').

The 'threshold of originality' question is a notable area in which the role of the EU, and in particular of the Court of Justice, can be decisive (see preceding section 'Threshold of originality'). This question of what constitutes originality is particularly relevant for cultural heritage organisations engaging in the production of effectively faithful surrogate copies of existing works in their collections. The harmonisation aims of the Union – and in particular of regulation such as the InfoSoc Directive – play a significant role in shaping how this question is addressed at EU level. At the time of writing (2017) it remains to be seen what effect the copyright legislation and judicial activities of the EU will have on former member states.

Licensing and open licences

Licensing

If a person wishes to undertake any of the restricted acts in relation to a work protected by copyright they may only do so under an applicable exception to copyright. If no such exception applies, or their intentions exceed what is permitted under the exceptions, they will require the permission of the copyright owner in order to proceed. Licences are the tool by which such permission is granted.

Only the owner of a copyright, or a person authorised to act on behalf of the owner, may issue a licence in relation to any particular work. A licence is a grant of permission to use monopolised property, often in a defined and limited way, and can therefore only be granted by someone who owns the property or is validly authorised to issue permissions related to that property. In the same vein, copyright licences can only be issued in relation to works in which copyright subsists. Works that are in the public domain cannot be licensed, because they do not contain intellectual property. Therefore, there are no intellectual property rights for any owner to justifiably monopolise. This is a pertinent matter for the cultural heritage sector, particularly in relation to the creation of 'surrogate' copies of public domain works (e.g. through digitisation or 3D modelling).

It is important to understand who owns a copyright and is therefore in a position to issue licences. A museum, library, archive or other body that owns a tangible artefact, such as a painting or a book, may very well lack ownership of the copyright in that work or any authorisation to act on the copyright owner's behalf. As a result, the organisation cannot issue licences in relation to the copyright in that work, and may be constrained in its own use of the item.

This premise naturally extends to others, such as individuals. If you go into a shop and purchase a copy of *The Da Vinci Code* you become the legitimate owner of the tangible artefact. As the owner of the tangible property, you are free to exercise your relevant rights, such as taking the book home, bending the spine, or even using it to prop open a door. However, it is obvious that by buying a copy of the book you do not take any ownership over the intellectual creation that has gone into *The Da Vinci Code*. You do not obtain any rights, therefore, in relation to the copyright subsisting in the work, and your use of the material continues to be bounded by such intellectual property rights. This is why you cannot legitimately copy the text of a book onto a website, for example. Your use of the intellectual property within the item, even if you own the material good, is bound by copyright and so must be limited to acts permitted under the exceptions to copyright or you must obtain permission through a licence.

Licensing, along with the existence of statutory exceptions, is the essential reaction to the presence of monopoly rights. Without the ability to grant permission the value of monopoly rights would be severely reduced. For example, for an author to fully retain their copyright, they would need to be a multi-disciplinarian, capable of being a printer, a publisher and a marketing executive. As few individuals have this array of skills it makes sense for authors either to assign or waive rights to others who have the means of printing, publishing and promoting their work.

Terminology and licensing elements

Listed below are definitions of some key terminology that is likely to be used in association with copyright licences.

Contract licence

A licence specifically granted and set out in writing. Creative Commons licences, the Open Government Licence, and other defined open licences are examples of this form of licence. Likewise, traditionally agreed contractual copyright licences, where two or more parties negotiate and agree a set of licensing conditions and sign a contractual agreement, are a type of contract licence. Contract licences are distinct from implied licences (see below).

Exclusive licence

A licence that is exclusive to the licensee. Only the licensee is permitted to use the relevant licensed material. Crucially, the licensor is also precluded from using the licensed rights where these are exclusively granted to a third party.[27] Open licences cannot by their nature be exclusive, since exclusive licences work counter to the principles of openness.

Implied licence

A licence that has never been formalised in writing or otherwise, but can be assumed to exist. According to the UK Intellectual Property Office, an implied licence may arise 'when all the circumstances suggest that the copyright owner expected the user to make use of the copyright material in the way they intend, even though this was never discussed and has not been written down anywhere', for example when a work has been created under commission but without particular agreement as to the use of the created work.[28] Relying on an implied licence may be a risky approach, since by its nature there is no specific evidence as to the existence of the licence and no iteration of the particular licensing conditions that apply.

Licensee

The recipient of the benefit of a licence. The licensee is the party granted permission to exploit the intellectual property in the licensed material.

Licensor

The party granting a licence.

Non-exclusive licence

A licence that is not exclusive to any one licensee. The licensor is within their rights to grant further licences in relation to the licensed material to other parties, and the licensor may themselves use the licensed material.[29] Open licences must be non-exclusive licences, because to be open a licence must apply to anyone with lawful access to the licensed material.

Non-revocable licence

A licence that cannot be arbitrarily revoked by the licensor during the term. Once granted, the licensee can benefit from the rights granted for the duration of the term, unless the licensor breaches the term of the licence.[30]

Perpetual licence

A licence that has no stated end date. Because copyright as a right is time limited, the intellectual licence granted in a 'perpetual' copyright licence expires at the same time as the copyright protection in the licensed work. Open licences, such as Creative Commons licences, are 'perpetual'.

Revocable licence

A licence that may be revoked by the licensor during the term for reasons other than a material breach by the licensee of the licence conditions.[31]

Royalty

A payment made by the licensor to the licensee in consideration of the rights granted under the licence.[32] A royalty may often be paid as a percentage of earnings or of returns generated through the use of the licensed material. Open licences cannot by their nature include a provision that requires payment of a royalty.

Royalty-free

A licence that is granted without the requirement to pay any royalty. A licence that grants free permission to the licensee.[33] Open licences need to be royalty-free by nature in order to be open.

Sole licence

A licence that is exclusive to the licensee, except that the licensor reserves the right to exploit their intellectual property in the licensed material. This is a rare form of licence, and may alternatively be construed by means of an exclusive licence with a specific caveat that the licensor may continue to exploit the intellectual property.[34]

Sub-licence

The further licensing of rights by a party other than the owner of the rights. Licensing undertaken by a licensee and done under licence of the initial licensor.

Term

The duration of a licence and/or duration of a copyright. The word 'term' is likely also to be used in the manner of 'terms and conditions' within a licence, so particular attention is required when this word appears.

Territory

The geographic region(s) in which the licence is applicable and in which the licensee is permitted to exploit the intellectual property under the licence.

Open licences

Open licences are a particular subset of licences, defined by the degree and scale of permission that they grant. There is no definitive list of 'open' licences, nor a single formal definition of what constitutes an open licence, although the Open Definition, prepared and maintained by the Open Knowledge International, provides a concise description of what is required of a licence in order that it be considered 'open'. The Open Definition defines knowledge to be 'open' so long as 'anyone is free to access, use, modify, and share it – subject, at most, to measures that preserve provenance and openness'.[35]

The application of an open licence to a work protected by copyright is one method of ensuring that, legally, the work meets this standard. The Open Definition goes on to specify nine elements a licence must irrevocably grant in order to be 'open' and lists seven areas in which a degree of limitation may be placed on those permissions. In summary, by this definition an open licence must be one that enables anyone to access, use, modify and share a work for free, with as little restriction as possible. The licence may require licensees to provide attribution and/or maintain the openness of the work while continuing to be considered 'open'; therefore restrictions do not place unwarranted or restrictive burdens on reusers.

The Open Definition is accompanied by a list of certain compatible open licences.[36] Six of these (at the time of writing) are listed as recommended open licences. Therefore licences meet the requirements of the Open Definition and are reusable, compatible and current. These factors are crucial to the usability and significance of open licences. Bespoke licences (e.g. those drawn up on spec by a licensor or licensee case by case) may, for example, meet any of the criteria of being 'open', such as by permitting free use and reuse without any obligation above the need to attribute the source. However, such bespoke licences are likely to be limited in scope to a small number of applicable works (as is the case for standard, bespoke licence agreements). This creates problems for any onward use of the licensed works or, more specifically, works derived from them. The power of standardised and generalised open licences, like those recommended by the Open Definition, is that they can apply to any copyright work and any user, and be applied by any copyright owner to their licensable works.

Creative Commons licences

Creative Commons licenses are perhaps the best known set of open licences for creative works. The suite of licences created and maintained by Creative Commons are nearly ubiquitous. In their report *State of the Commons* in 2015, Creative Commons stated that in excess of one billion copyright works have been made available under one of their licences.[37]

Creative Commons licences are modular in construction and each is presented in machine-readable, lawyer-readable and user-readable formats. The real 'licence' is the legal code (the 'lawyer-readable' layer), which takes the form of a fairly standard looking block of legal text. This is supported and interpreted by a non-binding user interface, which describes the licence in more approachable, everyday terms. These terms are further distilled to simple pictograms detailing the particular elements that make up the licence.

Creative Commons licences are, in short written form, normally referred to as 'CC' followed by a series of two letter abbreviations for the particular modules selected for the licence, as well as a number to indicate which version of the licence has been used (in some cases a region is then also specified, indicating that a 'ported' licence with jurisdiction-specific legal code has been used). For example, the unported version 4 of the Attribution ShareAlike licence is denoted 'CC BY-SA 4.0'.

According to *State of the Commons* in 2016 65% of the works available under one of their licences are provided through one of the 'free culture' licences. These three licences – CC Zero, CC BY and CC BY-SA – are the most open and permissive available from Creative Commons and enable free reuse for commercial and non-commercial purposes, including the creation and publication of modifications to the original work.

There are five modular elements, the absence or presence of which broadly make up the different licences that Creative Commons has made available. These modules are Attribution, ShareAlike, NonCommercial, NoDerivatives and Zero.

Attribution (BY)

This module requires that any use or reuse of the licensed content must be accompanied by credit and a link to the licence. This is the most pervasive module, and is present in all Creative Commons licences except for the zero licence: 97% of the approximately 1.1 billion works licensed under Creative Commons (by 2015) require attribution. Attribution is a low barrier to reuse and serves to ensure protection of the key authorial moral right to be recognised as the creator of a work. This module is arguably also one of the most important for the cultural heritage sector, as it can be a tool to help ensure that creator and source names are promulgated.

ShareAlike (SA)

This module requires that any new work that remixes, transforms or builds on the licensed work must be shared under the same licence or under one of the licences that Creative Commons lists as compatible. This module is synonymous with the 'copyleft' method of openly sharing modifications to content.[38] As of 2015, around half of all the Creative Commons licensed works were published with one of the two licences containing the SA module: CC BY-SA and CC BY-NC-SA. The CC BY-SA was the most common licence type of any of the Creative Commons suite, having been used with more than 35% of all Creative Commons' licensed works. Contributors to Wikipedia publish their work under the CC BY-SA licence.[39] There is value in using this module to ensure that open works remain open and foster more open works. However, this module can present serious challenges to onwards reusers of content who wish to generate new works and adaptations from material that has been licensed under incompatible SA licences.

NonCommercial (NC)

This module requires that any use or reuse of the licensed content may not be for commercial purposes. This module can be appealing for licensors wishing to undertake 'open licensing light', as well as those interested in or obliged to protect certain commercial interests. As of 2015, 20% of works licensed with a Creative Commons licence are subject to the NC module.[40] The application of the NC module prevents the licence from being considered a 'free content' licence by Creative Commons, but continues to enable the gratis reusability of the content for a range of non-commercial purposes.

NoDerivatives (ND)

This module requires the licensor not to distribute any modifications to the licensed work. The ND module is the most restrictive and least used of those provided by Creative Commons. Only 16% of Creative Commons licensed works (by 2015) used the CC BY-ND or CC BY-NC-ND licences.

Zero (CC0)

The Creative Commons Zero tool is a copyright waiver. Unlike the six other licences maintained by Creative Commons, the CC0 tool serves to surrender all rights that an owner derives from copyright control, including moral rights (e.g. of attribution as the author) so far as legally possible. This is the most liberal option. The Zero tool is the precise opposite of the all-rights-reserved position. A work released under the CC0 tool can be used, reused and adapted by anyone for any purpose, without obligation. Fundamentally, this is a tool for works that are protected by copyright, so in effect it is a licence (if not one in the traditional sense, since no rights are retained by any party). This tool may not be applied to works that do not benefit from copyright protection or no longer have copyright protection. See section 'Public domain mark', below.

For example, Europeana's Data Exchange Agreement requires all metadata submitted to Europeana by contributor organisations to be available under a CC0 dedication.[41] This requirement relates to the metadata themselves, not the data to which the metadata refer.

Public domain mark

This is not a licence, but rather a marker that Creative Commons has developed to help communities label and identify works that are in the public domain. Crucially, this mark cannot be applied to a work that is subject to copyright protection. If the owner of a copyright wishes to waive all of their rights in and to a work they can use the Creative Commons Zero tool (see section 'Zero (CC0)' above). By definition, therefore, unlike the six licences and one copyright waiver maintained by Creative Commons, this mark cannot be applied to a work by its copyright owner, because by definition no such party exists. Equally, unlike the licences and waiver tool, the mark does not serve to change the legal position of a work. An item is intellectually in the public domain when it is not eligible for copyright protection or when its copyright protection has expired. This is the case irrespective of whether it has been given a public domain mark or label. Unlike a licence, the public domain mark serves as an indicator alone and merely helps to highlight instances where a work is understood not to benefit from existing copyright protection. See section 'The public domain', page 60, for more information about the nature of the public domain and works falling outwith copyright protection. Figure 3.1 shows the Creative Commons licence spectrum.

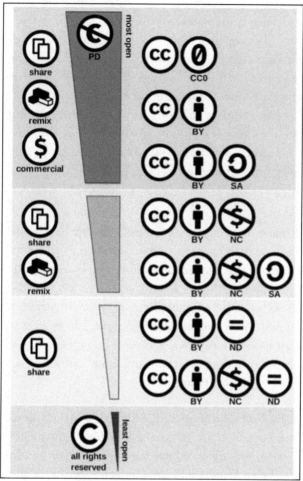

Figure 3.1 *Spectrum of Creative Commons licences from most open to most closed*
Source: https://commons.wikimedia.org/wiki/File:Creative_commons_
license_spectrum.svg

The Open Government Licence

A number of open licences have been created by and for public sector information. In the UK, The National Archives (successor to the Public Record

Office) has responsibility for Crown copyright and for public sector licensing, in accordance with the Re-use of Public Sector Information Regulations 2015 (PSI Regulations).

To facilitate open reusability of public sector information, The National Archives maintains the Open Government Licence as part of the UK Government Licensing Framework.[42] Currently in its third version, the Open Government Licence is the successor licence to the Click-Use Licence. The licence permits the copying, publishing, distribution, transmission and adaptation of information for commercial or non-commercial purposes, subject only to the requirement to acknowledge the source of the information and provide a link to the licence.[43] Some information is exempt from coverage of the licence, such as personal data and insignia. The Open Government Licence is compatible with the Creative Commons Attribution (CC BY) licence.

The Open Government Licence – Canada is effectively similar to both the UK's Open Government Licence and the CC BY licence.[44]

Other licences

Other open licences for copyright-protected content have evolved over time. Many grew up in relation to specific types of content, such as the Open Audio Licence published by the Electronic Frontier Foundation (EFF) in 2001.[45] A number of these specific licences have lapsed or declined and have been replaced by more broadly applicable licences, primarily those maintained by Creative Commons. An audio work, for example, can be licensed as easily by any of the Creative Commons licences as can a literary or dramatic work. There continue to be various non-Creative Commons and non-open government licences in use, however, including:

- *The Open Data Commons licences*, maintained by Open Knowledge International, operate to license databases, which in many jurisdictions are protected by both copyright and database right.[46] There are three licences in this suite: the Open Database Licence, which is broadly akin to a CC BY-SA licence; the Attribution Licence, which is broadly akin to a CC BY licence; and the Public Domain Dedication and Licence, which is broadly akin to a CC0 dedication. These three licences conform with the Open Definition.
- *The GNU Free Documentation Licence* is an open 'share alike' or 'copyleft' licence.[47] The licence accompanies the GNU General Public Licence, which is a comparable 'share alike' open licence for software.

- *The Free Art Licence* is another 'share alike' or 'copyleft' open licence that gives broadly comparable terms to a CC BY-SA licence.[48] In contrast to its name, there is nothing within the licence terminology that restricts its use to artistic works.

Assignation

As a property right, it is perfectly possible to transfer ownership of copyright. Indeed, given that copyright protection normally survives the creator of a work (who is normally the first owner of copyright) by several decades, it is inevitable that in many cases the final owner of a copyright is different from the original owner.

Assignation (or, 'giving') of copyright is not licensing. A licence is a grant of permission by an owner. Assignation, conversely, is a transfer of a right from an owner to a new owner (or owners). By assigning or giving copyright, the assignor (the party making the transfer) provides to the assignee (the party receiving the transfer) the rights afforded by copyright, namely the ability to enjoy monopoly control over the exercise of the restricted acts.

Assignation of copyright is largely comparable to the transfer of other property rights. For example, the owner of a table enjoys monopoly control over the use of that table. That person may transfer ownership of the table to someone else. This may be done, for example, through sale (transfer in exchange for financial compensation), through gift (transfer without direct reciprocity) or through inheritance (transfer through death). The new owner of the table now enjoys monopoly control over the table, and is in a position to exercise all the normal rights associated with ownership of a table (such as sitting at the table, allowing others to sit at the table, or even chopping up and rearranging the table). The original owner no longer owns the table, and as a result has relinquished the rights associated with ownership. The previous owner could not, for example, visit the new owner after the sale and begin sawing into the table.

Much the same situation applies to the economic rights derived from copyright. Once rights are transferred, the new owner of copyright enjoys monopoly rights over the exercise of the acts restricted by copyright, and the former owner ceases to enjoy them. A licence, on the other hand, no matter how permissive, does not transfer the ownership of any rights to another party.

Crucially, unlike economic rights, moral rights are non-transferable in the UK, but they are waivable. This means that the creator of a work may not assign their moral rights to another party. A new copyright owner is able to take full control of the economic rights associated with a work, even to the extent of excluding exercise of the restricted acts by the creator if the owner so wishes. However, the new owner is not able to obtain the moral rights, such as the right to be recognised as the author of the work.

The duration of copyright is normally associated with the lifespan of the author(s) of a work. Assigning copyright cannot transfer lifespan. Therefore, the author's date of death remains pivotal for establishing the duration of copyright (in relation to works where duration is associated with authorial lifespan).

Waiver

An act related to both licensing and assignation is the waiving of copyright. A total, and effectively permanent, surrender of all rights derived from copyright protection is known as a waiver. Unlike a licence, the copyright owner does not retain rights through this process and unlike an assignation no other party takes on the rights. However, like both a licence and an assignation, parties gain benefits in relation to the use of the relevant work, namely the right to undertake the acts restricted by copyright. The Creative Commons Zero (CC0) tool is a mechanism by which a copyright owner may indicate the waiver of all rights in and to a particular work.

Because a waiver is an act of discounting property rights, by definition only the owner of a copyright or a party authorised to act on the owner's behalf may waive a copyright. This is the same situation as a licence or an assignation. A copyright owner who is not the author of a work may waive all their economic rights in a work, but are unable to waive moral rights in the work, as these remain the property of the author. Moral rights may be waived in the UK, but only by the author of a work.

If the work is a work of joint ownership, a waiver of copyright by one author does not affect all rights in the work. A copyright waiver from all copyright owners is required in order to have the effect of removing all copyright protections.

The public domain

When the duration of copyright protection in a work expires the work enters the 'public domain'. Although through statutory changes it is possible for copyright protection to be revived after expiration, the underlying principle of copyright is that protection is time limited. This is in contrast to other forms of property, such as the ownership of tangible goods, which have no defined expiration and may technically remain in monopoly ownership in perpetuity.

When an intellectual work enters the public domain, there is no longer a right for any person to exercise monopoly control over the acts restricted by copyright in relation to that work. Therefore, once all relevant copyright has expired, anyone who has lawful access to the work or a copy of the work is able to undertake acts such as copying, transmitting or adapting the work without the need to seek permission or act within the confines of an exception. Nevertheless, because copyright is separate from tangible property, there is no guarantee that once intellectually in the public domain a work will materially be so. For example, an individual may own the only existing copy or copies of a work. The duration of copyright in that work may expire while the item(s) are in the person's possession. The work therefore intellectually enters the public domain. The material owner, however, is under no obligation to place the tangible item into the public domain, or even allow anyone else physical access to it. It is therefore important to bear in mind that intellectual and material access can continue to exercise distinguishable barriers to the use and reuse of a work, even when copyright has lapsed.

A work that is intellectually in the public domain may not be licensed, just as a work that does not qualify for copyright protection may not be licensed (in a copyright sense). Any rights granted by a copyright licence will expire no later than the time at which the copyright protection expires (although they may, by terms within the licence, expire sooner). This can be particularly significant in the case of exclusive licences, as by definition the exclusive control exercised by the licensee will expire along with the copyright (assuming it was not established to expire earlier).

Notes

1   Gov.UK, Intellectual Property and Your Work, n.d., www.gov.uk/intellectual-property-an-overview/protect-your-intellectual-property.

2   National Archives, History of Patents, 2012, http://webarchive.nationalarchives.gov.uk/20100202100434/ipo.gov.uk/p-history.htm.

3   Musk, E., All Our Patent Are Belong To You [sic], Tesla UK, 12 June 2014, www.tesla.com/en_GB/blog/all-our-patent-are-belong-you; IBM News Room, IBM Pledges 500 US Patents to Open Source in Support of Innovation and Open Standards, news release, 11 January 2005, https://www-03.ibm.com/press/us/en/pressrelease/7473.wss.

4   Musk, All Our Patent Are Belong To You [sic].

5   Intellectual Property Office, Case Details for Trade Mark UK00000000001, 8

October 2012, www.ipo.gov.uk/tmcase/Results/1/UK00000000001.

6 Gov.UK, Apply to Register a Trade Mark, n.d., www.gov.uk/how-to-register-a-trade-mark/what-you-can-and-cant-register.

7 BBC News, At the Core of the Apple Dispute, 8 May 2006, https://web.archive.org/web/20070207031925/http://news.bbc.co.uk/1/hi/entertainment/4750533.stm.

8 Gov.UK, Register a Design, n.d., www.gov.uk/register-a-design/check-if-you-can-register-your-design.

9 Gov.UK, Design Number 4011900, 2009, www.registered-design.service.gov.uk/find/4011900.

10 Gov.UK, Design Right, n.d., www.gov.uk/design-right.

11 Primary Sources on Copyright (1450–1900), Statute of Anne, London (1710), n.d., www.copyrighthistory.org/cam/tools/request/showRecord.php?id=record_uk_1710.

12 Primary Sources on Copyright (1450–1900), Licensing Act, London (1662), n.d., www.copyrighthistory.org/cam/tools/request/showRecord.php?id=record_uk_1662.

13 Swarb.Co.Uk, *Walter* v *Lane*: HL 1900, 1 July 2015, http://swarb.co.uk/walter-v-lane-hl-1900/.

14 Curia, *Infopaq International A/S* v *Danske Dagblades Forening*, 16 July 2009, http://curia.europa.eu/juris/document/document.jsf?docid=72482&doclang=EN, para. 37.

15 BnF, L'œuvre de l'esprit et les droits attachés, Bibliothèque nationale de France, 16 May 2014, www.bnf.fr/fr/professionnels/principes_droit_auteur.html; Legifrance, Code de la propriété intellectuelle, Article L112-2, 1994, https://www.legifrance.gouv.fr/affichCodeArticle.do?idArticle=LEGIARTI000006278875&cidTexte=LEGITEXT000006069414.

16 BMJV, Gesetz über Urheberrecht und verwandte Schutzrechte (Urheberrechtsgesetz), § 2 (2), Bundesministerium der Justiz und für Verbraucherschutz, 1965, https://www.gesetze-im-internet.de/urhg/BJNR012730965.html.

17 Intellectual Property Office, Copyright Notice: digital images, photographs and the internet, November 2015, https://www.gov.uk/government/uploads/system/uploads/attachment_data/file/481194/c-notice-201401.pdf.

18 WIPO, Limitations and Exceptions, World International Property Organization, n.d., www.wipo.int/copyright/en/limitations/.

19 BAILII, *Hyde Park Residence Ltd* v *Yelland & Ors* [2000] EWCA Civ 37 (10 February), England and Wales Court of Appeal (Civil Division) Decisions, British and Irish Legal Information Institute, 2000,

www.bailii.org/ew/cases/EWCA/Civ/2000/37.html. Para. 38.

20 Bodleian Library, Copyright, 2016,
www.bodleian.ox.ac.uk/bodley/using-this-library/copyright.

21 CILIP, Copyright Poster, Chartered Institute of Library and Information
Professionals, 13 January 2015,
https://www.cilip.org.uk/research/topics/copyright/resources/copyright-poster.

22 Hargreaves, I., *Digital Opportunity: a review of intellectual property and growth*,
Department for Business, Innovation and Skills, 2011,
https://www.gov.uk/government/uploads/system/uploads/attachment_data/file/
32563/ipreview-finalreport.pdf.

23 WIPO, Berne Convention for the Protection of Literary and Artistic Works, World
Intellectual Property Organization, 1886, Article 9 (2).

24 WIPO, WIPO-Administered Treaties, World Intellectual Property Organization,
n.d., www.wipo.int/treaties/en/ShowResults.jsp?treaty_id=15.

25 WIPO, Inside WIPO, World Intellectual Property Organization, n.d.,
www.wipo.int/about-wipo/en/.

26 World Trade Organization, Overview of TRIPS Agreement, 2017,
www.wto.org/english/tratop_e/trips_e/intel2_e.htm.

27 Taylor Wessing, Licensing – Exclusive/Non-Exclusive/Sole, 2017,
https://united-kingdom.taylorwessing.com/synapse/commerical_exclusive_
nonexclusive.html.

28 Gov.UK, License, Sell or Market Your Copyright Material, 6 May 2014,
www.gov.uk/guidance/license-sell-or-market-your-copyright-material.

29 Taylor Wessing, Licensing.

30 Sidley, The Terms 'Revocable' and 'Irrevocable' in License Agreements: tips and
pitfalls, 2013, www.sidley.com/news/the-terms-revocable-and-irrevocable-in-
license-agreements-tips-and-pitfalls-02-21-2013.

31 Sidley, The Terms 'Revocable' and 'Irrevocable' in License Agreements.

32 The Law Dictionary, What is Royalty?, n.d., http://thelawdictionary.org/royalty/.

33 The Law Dictionary, What is Royalty?

34 Taylor Wessing, Licensing.

35 Open Definition, Open Definition 2.1, n.d., http://opendefinition.org/od/2.1/en/.

36 Open Definition, Conformant Licenses, n.d., http://opendefinition.org/licenses/.

37 Creative Commons, *State of the Commons*, 2015,
https://stateof.creativecommons.org/2015/.

38 GNU, What is Copyleft?, 2017, www.gnu.org/licenses/copyleft.html.

39 Wikimedia Foundation, Terms of Use, 2016,
https://wikimediafoundation.org/wiki/Terms_of_Use.

40   Creative Commons, State of the Commons, 2016,
      https://stateof.creativecommons.org/.
41   Europeana Professional, The Data Exchange Agreement, 2015,
      http://pro.europeana.eu/page/the-data-exchange-agreement.
42   The National Archives, UK Government Licensing Framework, n.d.,
      www.nationalarchives.gov.uk/information-management/reusing-public-sector-
      information/uk-government-licensing-framework/.
43   The National Archives, Open Government Licence for Public Sector Information,
      n.d., www.nationalarchives.gov.uk/doc/open-government-licence/version/3/.
44   Government of Canada, Open Government Licence – Canada, 11 March 2015,
      http://open.canada.ca/en/open-government-licence-canada.
45   Electronic Frontier Foundation, EFF Open Audio License: version 1.0.1, 21 April
      2001, web.archive.org/web/20040818074301/http://www.eff.org/IP/
      Open_licenses/20010421_eff_oal_1.0.html.
46   Open Data Commons, Licenses, n.d., https://opendatacommons.org/licenses/.
47   GNU, GNU Free Documentation License v1.3, 2016, www.gnu.org/licenses/
      fdl-1.3.html.
48   Copyleft Attitude, Free Art License 1.3, 2007, http://artlibre.org/licence/lal/en/.

Chapter 4

Open licensing: the logical option for cultural heritage

Introduction

In this chapter we suggest that an open approach to licensing in cultural heritage should be developed. Building on the developments in the open movement and the realities of intellectual property rights set out earlier in this book, we argue that there should be openness in the sector. We describe why organisations should consider being open, looking in detail at both the core benefits and potential risks of an open approach.

Acting with purpose: why are you making digital collections available?

Digital raison d'être

Informed and logical decision making should guide the work of cultural institutions. A visitor to an exhibition of abstract art might expect to see works there by Piet Mondrian. Conversely, if the art of J. M. W. Turner was included it would appear out of place and visitors would reasonably question the decision making and structure behind the show.

The need to act with purpose is equally present in the newer, less tangible, and more fluid realms in which cultural heritage organisations are increasingly operating. If an art gallery intends to undertake a digitisation project, it is reasonable to expect that staff make informed decisions about what material will be captured, to what quality standards, and in what format images will be retained. A gallery preparing a digital exhibition on abstract art may seek to digitise works by Mondrian. It may be questionable for the gallery to use the launch of an abstract art exhibition to digitise works by Turner.

Cultural and information organisations need to make logical, strategic and sustainable decisions before, during and after digital capture, considering why material should be captured, how it will be managed before and after capture, and who it is being captured for. In short, organisations need to consider their digital *raison d'être*.

Strategy

The 2013 Enumerate study of nearly 1400 European cultural heritage institutions found that most (87%) had a digital collection. However, only around a third (36%) of the institutions had a distinct digitisation policy. Slightly fewer (34%) of the organisations actually had an explicit policy for the use of their digital collections.[1] These figures indicate that while maintaining digital collections is common and increasingly common, only about one-third of institutions have dedicated policies on digitisation. While it has become a *de facto* role of cultural heritage institutions to collect and curate digital material, this position has grown up faster than the structure of policy surrounding it. This structure is as important to the sustainability and viability of this work as it is to institutions' more 'traditional' collecting, curating and preserving roles.

Staff in institutions must acknowledge this and ensure that digital materials are provided with a platform equitable to traditional collections. As digital collections become ubiquitous it is vital that policy and practice keep pace, so staff must understand the lifecycle of their digital materials, and manage them accordingly.

Developing a logical and strategic approach to managing the lifecycle of digital collections is not merely an exercise in policy making or governance. Without appropriate tangible collection frameworks, a library can easily stray into disjointed collecting (e.g. failing to collect works that relate to a strategic and agreed theme) or a gallery can develop exhibitions that do not have a defined target audience. These core functions must be identified and developed with logical and strategic care. Equitable diligence is needed in the digital realm. For example, 'It is not enough to be open, it's important to be seen to be explicitly open and easily accessible.'[2]

Digital disruption

Digital technology has presented a host of paradigm shifts, for the cultural heritage and information sectors as well as for the wider world. It is natural that such shifts have impacted on practices and principles within the creative and knowledge fields, as elsewhere. Nevertheless, these shifts cannot be excuses for abandoning structure or vision.

Before digital technology became ubiquitous the cultural sector had a comfortable and established role in the creative and knowledge value chains. Cultural heritage organisations have historically worked:

- to identify content where it already exists
- to collect content in line with a defined strategy (e.g. to collect primarily modern art or primarily published medical texts)
- to provide access to the collections for current generations (e.g. within a gallery or reading room)
- to preserve the collections for generations to come (e.g. by regulating temperature in storage areas and raising the funds required to keep the lights on).

Organisations nurtured and encouraged further creation, but were rarely if ever generators or promulgators of works themselves.

Digital technology has disrupted this. A significant new role for organisations is to create digital copies of physical collections and to make them available to new and wider audiences. Organisations have long promoted collections and encouraged far-flung audiences to access them. The lending and loaning of works, as well as their sale and exchange, are by no means new practices. Similarly, it has been practical for several decades to facilitate the small-scale reproduction of works, where permitted by copyright, especially in paper-based organisations like libraries and archives. However, the ability for institutions, large and small, specialist and generalist, to facilitate the extensive and occasionally even *en masse* digitisation of material – as well as the digital distribution of digitised and born-digital works – is recent and groundbreaking to many established methods and mindsets.

Digitisation of material works can turn cultural heritage institutions, in part, into content publishers and distributors. These are roles that, by and large, libraries, archives, galleries and museums are not historically associated with or necessarily accustomed to. It is worth stressing these organisations are only, in this respect, 'a form' of publisher or distributor, since we are speaking about what is effectively the re-publication or re-issuing of works in a new medium. Today a gallery can take a painting of virtually any size, or an archive can take a volume of correspondence, and transfer the data contained in the paint or the ink into digital bits. The institution is then the curator not only of an original cultural artefact but also of its digital surrogate. Unlike the original, which the organisation rightly has a duty to retain and preserve *in situ* (save for occasional loans, perhaps), digital surrogates can be published, disseminated, manipulated, shared, transferred, transformed, edited and used in many other ways that a single, material original simply never could be.

This capability presents cultural organisations with a raft of exciting new opportunities as well as responsibilities and challenges. It is vital that due consideration is afforded to these responsibilities, and that benefits and challenges are assessed properly and accounted for appropriately.

Framework for the digital lifecycle

Gathering, generating, hosting, storing and providing access to and interpretation of digital material is neither free nor of marginal cost. Cultural heritage professionals and their funders would be somewhat astounded if the results of the Enumerate survey were translated to material collections. Can you imagine only around one-third of European cultural institutions having a distinct collecting policy or access policy?

Irrespective of what your organisation's digital *raison d'être* is, we suggest you assess and identify it from an early stage. You should aim to provide the same structure to your digital collection lifecycle as to your material or traditional collections. This involves considering why you have a digital collection, how you will develop and maintain it, who the digital collection is for, now and in the future, and what benefits you aim to realise through your investments in digital technology.

At the core of any cultural heritage or information sector strategy is likely to be access and use. Access to material and the onward use of that material is central to the organisational *raison d'être* of most institutions. In the analogue world 'access' often means visiting galleries or reading rooms, while 'using' means observing, consulting, noting and sketching. Access and use are also key considerations for digital strategies and plans. In fact, in many respects the consideration and development required here is greater than for other aspects of digital collection management. This is not because digital access and use require greater investment (far from it), but because digital access – and, by extension, use – present possibly a great paradigm shift for the culture and information sector compared with 'traditional' access and reuse approaches.

As we will explain, actively maintaining and perpetuating an open digital access and use environment is likely to be the most logical and strategic approach for the majority of institutions. The salient point is that assessing your digital *raison d'être* in the round must be active and conscious. The default position for intellectual property rights, as outlined in the previous chapter, is for maximum protection. As your collections are exposed to greater and more complex intellectual property rights structures in the digital sphere, the need to make clear and proactive choices is paramount. This is a stark contrast to the material environment, where routine access and use can largely be accommodated within the confines of default intellectual property positions. Therefore, it is essential that managers are able to assess their digital access and use procedures and identify their desired outcomes and benefits. We advocate that organisations do this using the established theme of 'openness'.

Why 'open'?

The logical and appropriate approach for cultural institutions managing digital content is to be 'open'. More than other sectors or fields, the provenance of culture and information management has been open. These foundations should be built on and perpetuated in the digital environment. The proper use and application of open licences provides a fundamental bedrock to an open approach. The information and cultural heritage sectors have clear and historical associations with 'openness', including an emphasis on access, sharing, use and non-discrimination between parties. The 'creation of the museum as an idea was heavily directed by the desire to make private collections accessible to and in the trust of the public domain'.[3] The prevailing *raison d'être* of the cultural heritage sector is the curation, preservation and promulgation of creative, scientific, historical, social and knowledge outputs. The sector is premised on and rooted in the generation and exchange of ideas and information. The natural ethos and outlook for the sector to adopt in the digital realm is openness.

The paradigm shifts of digital technologies have widened the 'open' mantle, which has been seized on by fields as diverse as education, governance and manufacturing, as set out in Chapter 2. A reinjection of contemporary concepts of 'open' into cultural institutions is timely and necessary, and likely to benefit organisations, users and content creators.

The cultural and information sectors are seeded in content creation, access and use. Operating institutions and policies that are open is at the core of what we do. Being open, in particular within the digital sphere, is logical, practical, economic and beneficial, considerably more so than contrasting closed positions. Information and culture institutions should adopt an open approach by default, as explained in the remainder of this chapter and illustrated in the case studies.

Legal and policy context

An open approach is in part about conforming to organisational, cultural, strategic or ethical criteria. However, there are also legal and policy considerations that can make an open approach more appealing and beneficial. Although regulation and policy apply in various ways to all actors, when considering open culture and the use of open licences this is particularly relevant for public organisations and those dealing in faithful reproductions of works that are themselves intellectually in the public domain (out-of-copyright and related rights).

Public organisations

Culture and information organisations that are funded wholly or in part by public investment, including many museums, galleries, libraries and archives, naturally have a duty to ensure their work maximises, or does not inhibit, public benefit. This often leads to practices such as opening collection areas to public exhibition (whether charged or free at the point of access), engaging in collaborative research projects, or lending expertise and experience to peer organisations and communities.

There is logic to an organisation producing or maintaining digital collections at public expense, maximising potential public return. This may be through enabling online access, or through investment in digital asset management and preservation infrastructure. As with material collections, public benefit may not always be synonymous with wide, contemporaneous access. For example, an archive may retain digital records that contain sensitive personal data of living individuals. The archive is likely still to be fulfilling its public duty by preserving those records, even while limiting or denying contemporary access. That said, many materials contained in public collections are not subject to these sorts of restrictions.

Council Directive 2003/98/EC on the reuse of public sector information (the PSI Directive) and its 2013 revision are transposed into UK law by the Re-use of Public Sector Information Regulations 2005 and 2015 (the PSI Regulations). The 2005 PSI Regulations specifically excluded from their scope information held by libraries, museums, galleries and comparable cultural organisations. These institutions were brought into scope with the 2015 PSI Regulations.

The PSI Regulations place certain criteria on the ways in which public organisations can and should enable the reuse of public information – the use by any party of information (in any form and format) generated or held as part of an organisation's 'public task' for further purposes. In general, the regulations ensure that public information that is available for reuse may be reused by anyone for any purpose on equitable terms ('non-discrimination'). The regulations do not require museums, libraries and similar organisations to make their public information reusable, but once an item is made reusable it needs to be reusable by others on equitable terms.

The PSI Regulations permit organisations to apply 'reuse conditions' – licence terms and reuse fees – and places particular restrictions on how these may be determined and levied. In particular, to ensure non-discrimination, 'reuse conditions' cannot vary between parties requesting comparable reuse of a particular piece of public information. At a basic level, for example, a library could not charge two external parties two different reuse fees for broadly the same type of reuse of the same public information (such as a digital image). Indeed, any fee the organisation chooses to charge for reuse needs to be calculated in accordance with the organisation's costs associated with enabling that reuse, plus a reasonable return on investment if desired. Fees are not obligatory and are actively discouraged by the regulations or prohibited outright for some organisations.

Significantly, the regulations also require that libraries, museums and other public organisations comply with their own reuse terms when reusing their own public information. This does not cover use of public information for purposes that are within their public task, but does cover further activities. For example, many organisations have a public task to collect, preserve and provide access to cultural works, but often do not have as part of their public remit the responsibility to run commercial sales operations.

If a public cultural organisation is considering applying reuse restrictions on public information not subject to third party copyright or other external restrictions, it needs carefully to consider the impacts and effects of the PSI Regulations and to ensure that its reuse framework remains compliant. It is possible to comply with the regulations while maintaining a closed reuse structure, but this can become challenging and complex for the organisation and its users. An organisation needs to consider whether by imposing reuse conditions it restricts its own potential reuse. For example, if a museum decides to apply restrictive licence terms and levy reuse fees for use of images in commercial products, that museum needs to be prepared to charge itself that same fee and comply with the same licence terms if it later hopes to make and market commercial products that use its images, on the reasonable assumption that the sale of goods is beyond the museum's public task. Additionally, organisations need to ensure that their licensing terms and reuse fees meet the regulations' requirements. For example, an institution should be able to demonstrate the basis on which any reuse fees have been calculated, in order to clarify that the amount charged relates to the organisation's costs for actually enabling that reuse.

The PSI Regulations require certain information about reuse conditions to be made available publicly, for example on an institution's website. It is important for institutions that place reuse restrictions on their public information to explain and justify this, in accordance with the regulations' transparency requirements.

Faithful reproductions of public domain works

There was a discussion in the previous chapter about making faithful reproductions of public domain works from a UK legislative standpoint. There remains considerable legal ambiguity as to whether a faithful two-dimensional reproduction of a two-dimensional work meets the 'threshold of originality' required to obtain copyright protection.[4] If the threshold is met, then the new surrogate work has copyright protection from the moment it is created (assuming the underlying work was not infringed in the process). If the threshold is not met, there is no fresh copyright in the surrogate. Although this uncertainty is pertinent whether or not the underlying source work (e.g. the painting) is in- or out-of-copyright, it is perhaps more pressing when the source work is in the public domain (out-of-copyright).

There are a number of possible scenarios, depending on how this originality question is answered:

- An in-copyright work is faithfully reproduced and the reproduction meets the threshold of originality.
- An in-copyright work is faithfully reproduced and the reproduction does not meet the threshold of originality.
- A public domain work is faithfully reproduced and the reproduction meets the threshold of originality.
- A public domain work is faithfully reproduced and the reproduction does not meet the threshold of originality.

In the first two cases, use of the surrogate is limited by any reuse restrictions on the source work. For example, if a gallery digitises a contemporary painting with the permission of the copyright owner, the gallery's ability to publish copies of the surrogate, enable reuse of the surrogate copies, and otherwise use the surrogate is first and foremost constrained by the permission it has from the owner of copyright in the painting. In this situation, it is still important to consider the legal questions around the threshold of originality in faithful reproductions, but the immediacy of the issue is reduced compared with the other scenarios.

In the second two cases, there are no rights existing in the source work. For example, if a gallery digitises a painting by Rembrandt (d. 1669) there is no copyright extant in the source work on the assumption that the work in question is a 'published' work in copyright terms. In these scenarios, the question of whether the surrogate copy attracts its own, new copyright protection attains greater significance. Unlike the first two scenarios, in these cases there are no intellectual property restrictions on the use and reuse of the source item. Thus, any such restriction placed on the surrogate can only relate to rights that may exist in the surrogate itself (in the digital file of Rembrandt's work, rather than in Rembrandt's own painting).

While it is beyond the scope or capacity of this book to rule on the threshold of originality question, it is important that the matter is taken into consideration by any organisation maintaining faithful reproductions of public domain works (see Chapter 3). Understanding this can have a major impact on how viable and sustainable your digital reuse framework may be. An organisation is more likely to develop an appropriate and durable reuse framework, with the most apt use of licences and rights statements, if this matter is addressed openly and honestly. Given the legal uncertainty, it is also prudent to remain attuned to case law and legislative developments, and to be prepared to adapt your policies or understandings accordingly if the legal position is altered or more clearly affirmed.

The arguments in favour of seeing these reproductions as not being subject to fresh copyright are strong, if as yet inconclusive. Note, in particular, the section 'Threshold of originality' in Chapter 3, discussing authors' intellectual creations. Proper use of licences and rights statements are therefore important, in order to communicate clearly to third parties the rights and reuse status of content in all forms. However, an organisation that feels it should or will exert copyright control over such reproductions is best to do so with due care and consideration on the understanding that the legal position, particularly in the UK and Europe, remains debatable. It takes either a change in the copyright *acquis* or a judicial decision at a suitably high level (e.g. in the Court of Justice of the European Union) to begin to resolve this issue. That said, organisations should remain mindful of the direction in which peer institutions are moving, the way in which the law is liable to move, and their further obligations and objectives.

The benefits of an open approach

Depending on the depth and degree of openness adopted, the material that has been opened and the actors involved, the benefits of an open approach vary. To some, the benefits of open cultural collections may only be marginal or remote, while to others benefits may be direct and significant.

When there is openness to culture and information there are six overarching benefits that are likely to result, at least in part, relating to: impact, availability, creativity, simplicity, the advance of knowledge at marginal cost, and the promotion of understanding and respect for copyright.

Material that has a higher potential for impact has wider, more even availability and is more likely to contribute to fresh creativity. Processes that are simple maximise benefit at marginal cost and advance respect for copyright and reuse restrictions.

Impact

Openness lowers the barriers to access and reuse. Lower barriers increase the potential for access and reuse. An increased potential for access and reuse brings an increased opportunity for impact, as well as more opportunity to demonstrate the significance and value of that impact to funders, donors or sponsor organisations. Making material open is therefore pragmatic and strategic.

Use of content on Wikipedia and other Wikimedia Foundation projects is one example of how open practices can generate rapid and quantifiable increases in reach, which can in turn be used to illustrate increased potential for impact from your collections, investments and efforts. Wikipedia is in the top ten of the most visited websites in the world.[5] The web domain of the Metropolitan Museum of Art in New York, by contrast, is ranked around 14,800th, the British Library's domain 21,500th, and the Rijksmuseum's 83,500th.[6] Therefore an organisation's content has a greater chance of access, use and impact if it is reachable via Wikipedia than if reachable by an institutional website alone. To be reached on a Wikimedia site, content must be 'free', either openly licensed or in the public domain.[7]

A simple way for institutions to generate greater reach via Wikipedia is to release openly licensed and public domain images to Wikimedia Commons, the repository holding images used on Wikipedia's articles. In 2015 the National Library of Wales began an active and concerted effort to expose open images from their digitised collection to Wikimedia Commons (see case study, Chapter 7). Over a six-month period between February and July 2015, there were an average of 177,805 views of Wikipedia and other Wikimedia web pages containing images from the Library's digitised collections. During the same six-month period in 2016, that average rocketed to 13,617,585, a more than 76-fold increase.[8] The reason for much, if not all, of this increase was that more images from the Library were made available on more Wikipedia pages. This was only possible because open principles had determined the organisation's non-restricted digitised content.

While these figures do not suggest that the Library's images are, per se, being used and reused more, or are necessarily having a greater impact, they clearly show that the Library's content is gaining wider exposure, and therefore has a much higher potential to generate impact. Significantly, this quantum leap in potential was obtained in a short period of time through basic principles of opening content, rather than through disruptive or costly efforts to construct new premises or develop new web features.

A higher potential for impact naturally has major and positive implications for the growth of knowledge and creativity, but can also derive more immediate benefits for the institutions that release material. In an era of contracting budgets and increased demands it is important for any public service to be able to demonstrate value and impact. Organisations hoping to secure or increase funding may wish to isolate 'tangible proof-points' of their demonstrable impact and value.[9]

One way of doing this is to capitalise on the latent value in digitised collections by ensuring these are, wherever possible, made actively and purposefully open. Openness, quite simply, enables the faster and cheaper availability of information than would otherwise be possible. Organisations do not need to build a new Wikipedia. By opening content, organisations can ensure their existing works are more likely to be available through already popular destinations, and by capturing and reporting figures can demonstrate to funders that investment in making collections digital and open can reap considerable rewards in reach and potential for impact. Openness enables institutions to place existing assets where the users already are, at marginal cost and effort.

Availability

Openness allows content to be shared and disseminated more easily, seamlessly and effectively than if it remains closed. For example, limiting the sharing and use of images and other content in order to protect the ability to exploit commercial reuse is rational from a restrictive point of view. From a cultural heritage and information point of view, however, it is not rational. Withholding the 'best' assets with the aim of releasing them only under bespoke licences cripples the ability to share with audiences, and potential audiences, just how exceptional the content is. The more optional barriers are erected, the more unneeded limits are placed on an organisation's own chances of success. In an age when sharing, connectivity and choice are abundant, the logical home for non-profit knowledge and cultural organisations is at the forefront of openness, shouting loudly about collections, without concern for artificial limitations. The age of connectivity is the ideal opportunity to capitalise on technology and use it to ensure collections are as accessible and available as possible.

Europeana estimates that there are around 300 billion cultural 'objects' in Europe, but that only around 3.4% of these have been digitised and made available online.[10] Incredibly, just 0.3% of these 300 billion objects have been digitised and had their digital surrogates made available openly for use and reuse. In an era that we think of as digital, it is surprising to realise that only a tiny proportion of our cultural heritage is openly reusable in digital form. Naturally, much of our cultural heritage does not lend itself to digitisation. The Enumerate study estimates around 30% of the cultural heritage in European institutions does not require digitisation.[11] Plenty of content has been generated in recent decades and so is subject to copyright-based restrictions. Some content is subject to other restrictions, such as protection of personal data or restrictive material ownership terms. Nevertheless, there is a clear gap in the market for much greater generation of openly reusable digitised culture and information.

A persistent problem for cultural institutions has always been space and capacity. In the world of tangible information and cultural assets there is a real and low limit to the amount of data that can be imparted to visitors and users. Museums and galleries are rarely able to display all of their collections, the vast majority of works remaining for much or all of their lifetime in storage. The sector has long curated and preserved far more data and information than can be displayed or engaged with. While space restrictions persist in the digital environment, these are lower than in the physical world. Digitisation gives institutions a fresh opportunity to expose and provide access to this 'hidden' material, thus deriving greater value from investments already made in collection, interpretation and storage. Openness adds a further vital layer. By making digitised collections openly available organisations can expand their reach, because open collections have a greater potential to be used and shared.

Ed Rodley of the Peabody Essex Museum in Massachusetts urges us to think of the internet as a new continent, 'rapidly being populated by all sorts of ideas and content'. He argues that survival is much the same on this new continent as it is in evolution and depends, therefore, on the 'widest, most promiscuous spread of the cultural seeds we steward and create'.[12] There is an intuitive logic to this, seen for example in the boom and bust of the early world wide web. If organisations want to conquer this space and derive benefit through increased exposure, access and use, they need to narrow the gap between our billions of cultural objects and the minuscule percentage of these currently available for open, digital reuse. This requires adopting an open approach.

Creativity

The foundation of creativity is a combination of ingenuity and prior art. This is a fundamental principle on which the millennia-old establishments of schools and libraries are based. Access to material breeds creativity. Not only is creative endeavour a key foundation for cultural institutions themselves, but creativity has a vital role to play in wider society. For example, a 2010 survey of chief executives undertaken by IBM discovered that 'more than rigor, management discipline, integrity or even vision – successfully navigating an increasing [sic] complex world will require creativity'.[13]

Digitisation offers cultural heritage organisations the ability to expand their reach and potential to contribute to greater creativity. More people are able to access more collections, with greater ease and at lower cost (than, for example, travelling between far-flung reading rooms and galleries). Accessible content is key to fostering further innovation, and this is likely to be a core pillar in many digitisation efforts.[14] However, access is only a part of the puzzle. It is fundamental that our cultural heritage and accumulated prior art and knowledge are usable and reusable when they are accessible, in particular when the source material is no longer protected by copyright. This is akin to the 'free content' and open principles that underpin the wiki movement, world wide web and internet. 'New art rarely exists in isolation. Instead, new art is routinely built on the creative work of artists who came before. When a museum constrains the public domain, it is inhibiting new creativity and scholarly exploration.'[15]

Making public domain collections available through digitisation is an essential first step to widening access and promoting creative engagement. However, placing restrictions on their use and reuse places undue and illogical barriers in the way of genuine and prolific engagement.

Cultural heritage organisations thrive and rely on the presence of creativity and ingenuity. Without creation there simply would be no need for collecting organisations, not to mention a considerable dearth in the degree of social development. Making digital collections openly available for access, use and reuse greatly increases the opportunities for content to form a basis of further creativity. This acts as a mutually beneficial cog in the creative cycle, as collecting and heritage organisations enable the further creation of new works. Creativity is possible with closed material, but the barriers are greater and the opportunities lower.

Simplicity

Maintaining closed content is by default about implementing and enforcing restrictions. This requires the development of practices for authorising reuse, engagement of staff time in issuing permission and monitoring compliance, and generating procedures and policies around what may and may not be done with discrete types of content in excess of what is already required (e.g. by content depositors or third party copyright owners).

Speaking of the Rijksmuseum's much lauded release in 2013 of free-to-download high-resolution digital images, Taco Dibbits, Director of Collections, justified the museum's move in part by explaining 'With the Internet, it's so difficult to control your copyright or use of images that we decided we'd rather people use a very good high-resolution image of *The Milkmaid* from the Rijksmuseum rather than using a very bad reproduction.'[16] In other words, Dibbits and the Rijksmuseum realised that there was greater benefit in releasing their content than in forcing their users to nip around the edges, whether by copying images against the museum's policies or making do with lower quality derivatives.

There are various benefits. For example, if copies of your institution's works are repeatedly being used at an inferior quality, this may have negative implications on how the wider public views your collections. Seeing mostly or only poor copies of Johannes Vermeer's *Milkmaid* could lead people to think that the Rijksmuseum has not been looking after the original well, or does not take digitisation seriously.

However, there are also benefits in introducing simplicity, which in turn lowers costs and barriers. Before it allowed free reuse of its images, the Rijksmuseum would have needed to regulate reuse, generate and enforce permission for reuse, identify and (at least in theory) pursue unapproved reuse. Each of these activities generates added layers of complexity and cost to an already complex environment. Crucially, as Dibbits acknowledges, these obligations were self-imposed in relation to copies of public domain works. They were not necessary. By restricting reuse beyond the degree actually required, institutions generate for themselves and their users more complexity and cost than is likely to be required.

A digital cultural heritage environment where restrictions are isolated only to the degree and scope actually required is liable to be far simpler than one in which added layers of compliance have been added. Appropriate and concerted use of open licences and statements wherever possible is an important tool in ensuring that complexity and restriction are kept to an essential minimum. A simple, open environment should still ensure that when necessary works are protected, for example because of third party copyright, but avoids adding any further restrictions. In the Rijksmuseum example, allowing everyone to reuse the high quality copy of *The Milkmaid*, once the museum had such a copy, was simpler than making different users intending different reuses apply for or be subject to different reuse terms. Once the museum decided to allow anyone to reuse the image of *The Milkmaid* they were able to divest the monitoring, enforcing and gatekeeping responsibilities they previously hoisted on themselves of materials that could in reality be made openly available. Built into an organisational process with clarity and purpose, an open approach can enable these added layers to be dispensed with early on, or avoided from the start.

Advancing knowledge at marginal cost

An open approach to cultural content enables the spread of knowledge at a remarkably marginal cost. In the overall value chain of content creation, storage and consumption, the costs associated with openly sharing copies of works is extremely low. While technology advances are by no means entirely cost-beneficial or cost-neutral (e.g. while digitisation enables greater spread and stability of collections it also necessitates increased curation, management and storage as existing collections are effectively multiplied), removing unnecessary restriction layers comes at low cost and comparatively high potential for return.

Once a cultural organisation has created digital copies of a material work, the costs and obligations associated with maintaining that copy do not vary regardless of whether the derivative is made openly or restrictively accessible. Unlike analogue or tangible works, digital surrogates by their nature exist as copies, which are copied over and over again at no further cost. The organisation is not deprived of its digital copy when a user takes and uses an image, as that organisation would be deprived of a tangible object if a visitor took a painting away with them. Even in contrast to the world of mechanical copying, the margins are considerably lower with digital derivatives, as new digital copies do not require fresh ink, paper or moving parts. The added cost of open reuse, in excess of creating digital surrogates, is arguably zero for the organisation, since even the small amount of new storage space required for a fresh copy of the copy will be on the user's device, not on the institution's.

As with stimulating creativity, it should be in the inherent interests of a knowledge organisation to promote and foster the advancement of knowledge. In consideration that institutions by their nature undertake the immense work of collecting, storing and providing secure and sustainable access to material works and their digital surrogates, it seems entirely counter-productive to place unnecessary barriers to wide and ready use and reuse of that information at the final stage. Unwarranted restrictions on access and reuse, for example if placed unnecessarily on copies of public domain works, place a confusing and irrational block on the organisation's very mission as expressed through the efforts invested in content selection, curation and digitisation. Conversely, enabling open access and reuse wherever possible adds no additional costs or time to the organisation's processes, yet hugely increases the potential for those efforts to be capitalised on.

Promote understanding of and respect for copyright

While it is possible, through contract, to withhold and grant permission to obtain and use an item (as opposed to intellectual property that may or may not exist within that item), there has been frequent and messy tangling of material restrictions and intellectual property restrictions by organisations seeking to retain closed digital collections. Cultural institutions frequently label digital surrogates of public domain works as being the copyright of the institution, the argument being that the digital image (rather than the underlying work) is a new creative work worthy of protection (see section 'Threshold of originality' in Chapter 3). Even where organisations are less overt about asserting copyright control over public domain surrogates, it is common to find images released under Creative Commons licences, which are copyright licences, and in simple terms cannot be applied to works that are not in-copyright.

As discussed, it remains a matter of legal debate whether faithful reproductions of two-dimensional works are themselves worthy of copyright protection. However, irrespective of the legal conclusion, messy and confusing management of digital access and reuse by cultural institutions has wider negative implications. Poor and inconsistent use of copyright notices and licences can debase and devalue these tools in relation to works that genuinely require clear and restrictive terms (e.g. a digital copy of a contemporary work of art that has been copied under licence).

Seeking to restrict the reuse of openly accessible and available copies of works that are intellectually in the public domain, and often retained and managed at public expense, generates new and unwarranted layers of copyright complexity. Cultural heritage professionals and content creators know from experience that copyright is already complex, and the tome that is UK's Copyright, Designs and Patents Act 1988 is some testament to that. It is counter-productive for cultural heritage organisations to enforce fresh, unnecessary and complex barriers while trying simultaneously to encourage access to material and safe and proper use of works that contain existent third party intellectual property rights.

If cultural organisations hope to ensure their users understand copyright and are able to use contemporary collections in accordance with existing rights, then it follows logically that institutions should do all that they can to make these rights clear and to distinguish between open and closed works. It seems equally logical that organisations should attempt to do all within their power to make licences and rights statements as clear, consistent and fair as possible. This should be achieved through logical, purposeful and accurate application of openness, through proper use of licences and right statements.

The risks of an open approach

As with any practice, being 'open' has costs and negative risks as well as benefits. On the whole, however, the benefits outweigh the costs and negative risks.

We will not seek to outline a full range of risks that can occur through the introduction of an open approach. As with benefits, risks vary depending on the situation, the resources and the actors involved. Similarly, the degree and depth to which an open approach is embraced can have an impact. Benefits may fail fully to materialise if openness is only partly adopted, and in the same vein risks may be decreased or increased if openness is only partly pursued.

In this section we address what we feel are likely to be the most common and concerning risks. As well as outlining the sources of these risks, we explain how to mitigate these risks through purposeful and strategic action and how we believe that the negative impacts of these risks, if realised, are nevertheless outweighed by the positive impacts derived from the benefits of an open approach.

This section focuses on five sources of risk, which each derive from a potential loss:

- of income (the licensing risk)
- of control (the curation risk)
- of visits (the diffusion risk)
- of position (the competition risk)
- of aura (the dilution risk).

Loss of income – the licensing risk

Perhaps the most obvious, and possibly the most concerning, implication of removing restrictions on access and reuse is removing an opportunity to generate income. Selling downloadable images or issuing paid for licences to reuse digitised content are two of the most immediate ways in which digital content can be monetised by a cultural organisation. The practice is common. By definition, taking an open approach disrupts these streams. However, an open approach does not signify a no-income environment. Instead, with openness there is an opportunity to introduce greater nuance, justification and sustainability to income generation.

The licensing risk needs to be broken down and challenged in four distinct ways:

- *Clarity*: Digitised content sales and licensing is often messy, which derives from the shaky grounds on which the approach can often be based.
- *Income and relative loss*: It is worth considering in detail whether an organisation is generating income through restrictions and, if so, whether any of the income is profit and what the relative loss of this income would be.
- *Objectives*: It is important to understand what the objectives are for digital content and where reuse restrictions fit within those objectives.
- *Alternatives*: Reuse restrictions are not the only means by which digital content can be used for income generation – there are often viable alternatives that are less restrictive and may prove more rewarding.

Clarity

Generating direct income from restrictions on access and reuse of digital cultural content can be messy, especially when dealing with digitised surrogates of public domain works, because there are two things that a fee may be charged for:

- the right to obtain material (e.g. paying a fee to get a copy of an image)
- the right to reuse material (e.g. paying a permission fee to use an image in a publication).

And four sources of justification for levying fees:

- as owner of original or source material (e.g. a painting)

- as owner of derivative or surrogate material (e.g. a digital reproduction of a painting)
- as owner of intellectual property in original or source material (e.g. copyright in a letter)
- as owner of intellectual property in derivative or surrogate material (e.g. any copyright in a digital reproduction of a letter).

If a cultural organisation seeks to generate income through licensing, it must be clear to staff and customers from the outset what exactly is being licensed and under what justification(s). For example, it should avoid the befuddlement that greeted a tweet and blog post from the UK Intellectual Property Office in 2016, which purported to offer insights into how a gallery protected the copyright of William Shakespeare (who died in 1616).[17] The less that this is defined the greater the likelihood of uncertainty and the higher the potential for added cost (e.g. though protracted discussions and explanations). Therefore, if the reduction in income-generating potential is considered a negative risk, it is essential to understand whether the organisation is in fact able to restrict content for income potential in a manner that is justified and not overly opaque.

Income and relative loss

The second matter an organisation needs to examine is whether restrictions on access and reuse actually are enabling it to generate income, and if so whether any of the income generated is in fact profit. This is about distinguishing between the generation of income and the potential to generate income, as well as the distinction between the generation of profit and the generation of income 'at any cost'. This is closely linked to the matter of clarity, since the lower the degree of clarity the more likely it is that the organisation's costs will be higher than they should be, with a resulting negative impact on income and profit.

How much does it cost your organisation to put into place, regulate and enforce restrictions? How much do licensing activities cost your organisation? As part of its decision to enable free downloading and reuse of high quality images, the Rijksmuseum took into account the fact that they were unsure how much money and resources they actually spent generating income from image sales (which in 2012 amounted to an annual total of 0.2% of their overall level of income).[18]

The open approach does not imply that charges should never be made. For example, if an organisation needs to digitise an item or needs to reformat a digital file in order to meet a request, there are clear and tangible grounds for charging, if the organisation so wishes. However, where the content already exists in the format required, free from external restrictions, the added cost to the organisation of enabling reuse is effectively zero, up to the point that it decides to add a licensing layer. If applying restrictions, the organisation requires time to issue licences, legal resource to generate licence agreements, capacity to monitor misuse, and technical barriers to prevent misuse. None of this cost is required in relation to content that already exists and is free from external restrictions. Therefore, an organisation seeking to restrict this type of content for the purposes of generating income needs first to consider what costs it has to introduce to generate that income and second whether it can recover in charges more than it bears in fresh costs.

As the Rijksmuseum and others have discovered, the sums are a challenge. Attempting to regulate and control digital content, which you are likely also to be seeking to provide access to (see section 'Objectives', below), can be complex and expensive. Therefore, it is essential to consider whether a loss of income may be compensated for by a saving in otherwise unnecessary expenditure, as well as whether investments in generating income are in fact generating profit above and beyond the fresh costs you are incurring. To assess any of this effectively it is a prerequisite that you understand what you are restricting, on what basis, and by what justification.

Objectives

Irrespective of whether restrictions may or may not provide your organisation with reasonable income or profit, consideration needs to be afforded to your reason(s) for generating digital collections in the first place. Respondents to the Enumerate survey were asked to assess the importance (on a 1 to 10 scale, with 10 being 'most important') of seven reasons for providing digital access to collections. Academic research (scored 8.5/10) and educational use (scored 7.9/10) were ranked highest while 'sales and commercial licensing' was considered by far the least important (obtaining a score of just 3.2/10).[19]

This gulf illustrates how organisations are thinking about their digital collections' *raison d'être*, at least intuitively. This reality should call into question whether restrictions beyond those required through third party rights and contracts are indeed worthwhile. If an organisation's digital *raison d'être* is to promote access, are restrictions the most strategic choice? If image sales and licensing is on an organisation's digital agenda, but is ranked below other objectives, is the application of the restrictions required to enable sales and licensing actually inhibiting the proper exercise of its other, higher-ranked, objectives?

Alternatives

Finally, consideration of alternative methods of income generation is vital. While discussions of objectives and profit versus income are valid, these can nevertheless appear academic when there is a clear bottom line that costs need to be covered and income generated. Perhaps rightly, digital surrogates can be seen as assets, and so it may be undesirable to pass on them as an opportunity for income generation, even if at partial expense of other objectives.

However, it is unlikely that restrictions applied to enable income generation are the best or only way to cover costs or earn added revenue. Indeed, the presence of restrictions needed for generating permission fees may even preclude an organisation from properly exploiting other, less restrictive income-generating practices, especially when factors such as the PSI Regulations are accounted for. There is nothing to guarantee that every organisation will find secure or lucrative revenue streams from collections, but this can often be done to some degree. Importantly, activities such as selling items derived from collections, like books, posters or mugs, does not require that restrictions are placed on such content. An organisation has its collection from the start; it has its brand and position, and the curatorial expertise and knowledge of its staff. These are not lost when an open approach is adopted.

Loss of control – the curation risk

Being open is about relinquishing control. By placing information in the public sphere under open licences or reuse terms you are removing a layer of control that you might otherwise exert, whether through material or intellectual property, or both. The nature of the public domain is self-evident – information that is public – so no one person or actor has the right to exert monopolistic control over it.

If you have concerns about a loss or reduction in control over your collections, however, it is worth considering what this may actually mean in practice for your organisation and for others. For example, it is worth asking yourself:

- What actual control will be lost?
- What will we gain by retaining that control? What will our (potential) users gain if we retain control?
- If some control is lost, how will this damage us? Will it damage the material? The information's veracity? The public?
- Do we have the right to maintain this level of control over this particular material?

There are some clear cases where openness may result in negative loss of control, such as a library loaning out rare books or a museum permitting visitors to touch artefacts. However, when dealing with derivative digital copies of works, the potential for harm is different. In short, enabling open reuse of digital copies of works will not pose any threat to the physical integrity of the original item or your digital copy of it (since users will be dealing with copies of the copy, after all). In this sphere, therefore, any possible negative impacts from relinquishing control will be intellectual, moral or social in nature, not physical.

This is a significant distinction, and in part calls into question the role of culture and information organisations. The preservation of the material integrity of works in our care is clear, as is the role to preserve for the future the understood meaning of the works, or at least the ability of individuals to interpret meaning from the works. Is this degraded by allowing open reuse of copies of copies? It is entirely possible that a reuser will take an openly available derivative and use it for purposes that might be considered undesirable (whether for marketing a particular product, or promoting a particular ideology, or creating a new work based on an earlier one – think, for example, of Marcel Duchamp's *L.H.O.O.Q.*). However, do organisations have the right to attempt to prevent this from happening, provided that the original work is intellectually in the public domain and is not materially threatened (in the example of *L.H.O.O.Q.*, Duchamp's reworking of the *Mona Lisa* would certainly have been the prerogative of the Louvre to control had he attempted to draw a moustache onto the original as opposed to a postcard surrogate copy)?

Enabling open reuse of copies of public domain works does not necessitate giving permission, for example, to defame anyone or to generate hate material. Nor does it permit an individual to associate their work with the source organisation or imply that because the derivatives have been made openly available the source organisation in some respect endorses their efforts. However, it does allow individuals to do what they wish with the copies within the confines of the law, which is the precise intention of the public domain. It is questionable whether this reality is likely to present any genuine negative risks to a source organisation.

A separate negative impact that may be associated with a loss of control is the matter of provenance. By enabling open access and reuse, especially under fully open terms such as material given a public domain mark or dedication, organisations face the risk that content will be shared and reused without the source organisation (and/or content creator, source and so on) being attributed. This is perhaps a greater source of risk than those associated with perceived misuse of derivatives. Nevertheless, the implications of this risk should again be approached with caution. As well as questioning whether it is correct to require individuals to attribute the source institution in cases where they are reusing surrogate copies of public domain works, the active and pragmatic use of open licences and practices gives organisations the opportunity to help users cite their sources.

Taking the example of Vermeer's *Milkmaid*, Taco Dibbits cited his desire for anyone wanting to turn images of that masterpiece into toilet paper to at least do so with a good, high quality image. There are a couple of notable points here. The first relates to the reality that acts as undercurrent to Dibbits' statement: users were finding low-grade copies anyway. It is unlikely that those copies had robust metadata associated with them. By giving users the museum's own best copy, the Rijksmuseum also gave itself the opportunity to disseminate copies accompanied with good metadata (including provenance data) and to further develop the museum as the go-to source for images of the painting. The second matter to observe relates to the 'misuse' impact previously discussed. It is merely worth dwelling on Dibbits' acknowledgement that someone might wish to use a copy of a Dutch masterpiece for toilet roll.

Loss of visits – the diffusion risk

The converse effect of invigorating fresh engagement through external channels, such as Wikipedia, is that an organisation may fail to draw as many visitors to its own destinations, whether physical or digital. There are a couple of simple ways to address and mitigate against the impacts of this risk.

First, it is not clear that opening content causes visitor numbers to decline. In fact, a study in 2013 of open practices at 11 major American and British museums found that openness led to, or at least did not prevent, the number of visits to virtually all of the museums' websites increasing, in most cases by at least 100%.[20]

Second, negative impacts of this risk depend largely on what an organisation considers 'visitor success' to look like. Even if visits are reduced – which appears unlikely – organisations may still find success in looking to where those visitors are heading instead. In the case of the National Library of Wales, this would involve capturing the impressive level of potential exposure that its digital images have had since being published on Wikimedia Commons. An element of this might also be highlighting the diversity of the types of potential audiences the Library is able to reach, which is likely to be far wider on one of the world's most popular websites than on its own domain.

If the visitor facts and figures that matter to your organisation relate to how large and wide an audience it reaches, having an open approach presents more of an opportunity than a threat. Provided that your organisation is willing to capture exposure of its content as a 'visit' irrespective of whether it occurs in your building or when an item is on loan, whether on its website or where a digital object has been reused elsewhere, being open provides more opportunities to notch up visits and diversify your audiences.

Loss of position – the competition risk

The impacts that may derive from this risk are closely associated with those that may arise under the loss of control risk. When content is made open the possibility is introduced that another party will take the content and legitimately set up what might feel like a competing service. For example, this could involve displaying your organisation's digitised content on a private website or selling copies of your images.

Again, at a first pass the negative impacts of this risk appear significant. However, with greater consideration this risk is likely to be of minimal threat. In short, you should consider what a third party might be able to do with your content better than your organisation. If a third party is only liable to create a poorer version of your organisation's service they should not be viewed as a competitor. If they are truly liable to create a rival you have a few options. It may again be worth considering what the negative impacts of this really would be. After all, this will still represent opportunities for your collections and funded work to be making impact and being accessed, not to mention adding wider economic impact. Furthermore, it may well be that if this is a real threat, it can be pre-empted since the organisation retains various advantages, including being able to act first (you have the source material, after all) and being able to use your organisation's name and brand.

In fact, being open can provide advantages – if there is concern about competition, then your organisation's goal should be to create the best possible offering: be the go-to source for reusable material from your collections. An easy and cost-effective way of doing this is offering material at the highest possible quality with the fewest possible barriers. In the digital cultural heritage sphere the simplest and most effective way to achieve this is by adopting an open approach. Taking again the example of the Rijksmuseum's *Milkmaid*, Taco Dibbits felt inclined to release his organisation's best quality imagery for free in part because users were finding it easier to get copies (albeit, of inferior quality) elsewhere. People were going with the free, easy to obtain copies, despite the lower quality. Being open wherever possible will help your organisation remain relevant and pertinent to third parties, especially those that are liable to turn to the readiest source available.

Loss of aura – the dilution risk

This final risk is closely linked to the competition risk. Impacts of the dilution risk could arise through a perceived oversaturation of cultural objects or an environment wherein pervasive access to digital content, perhaps from third party sources (e.g. Wikipedia) as well as traditional or established sources, has dulled the 'aura' of works: 'that which withers in the age of mechanical reproduction is the aura of the work of art'.[21] Any direct negative impacts of this to source organisations would arise through what would effectively be a form of competition by the broader audience no longer finding uniqueness or value in the content being maintained by institutions.

The impacts of this risk seem highly unlikely to be realised, at least by applying an open ethic. In pure numerical terms, we are far removed from the cultural or information sphere being diluted by the presence of open content (e.g. given that only around 0.3% of extant European cultural objects are currently openly available in digital form). Indeed, even if we were to reach a point where this balance favoured openly accessible and reusable cultural works, it seems remote that this would have negative impact on the value, veracity or significance of the source objects or the culture and information spheres more generally. For example, as Deborah Ziska of the National Gallery of Art in the US notes, we have 'gotten over' the hurdle of worrying that cheaper reproduction of culture will necessarily dilute art and creativity.[22]

Reasons for retaining closed material

Organisations always have valid reasons for retaining 'closed' material that has not been exposed through open mechanisms such as the use of open licences. These should be identified and retained as part of the due assessment processes described here. The omission of openness by information cultural organisations should be specific and isolated, and not the default position. As with the application of open principles, and under the overarching theme of this chapter, the maintenance of 'closed' material should be logical, strategic and sustainable.

What does 'closed' mean?

By 'closed', we mean simply the opposite of 'open'. Material is 'closed' when it is not open for anyone to 'access, use, modify, and share', or, if it is, the barriers to doing so are steeper than a requirement to preserve provenance and openness. In other words, 'closed' material is any material that does not fit within the Open Definition.[23] It is worth distinguishing between semi-closed and fully closed material, particularly from a licensing perspective.

Fully closed material

Fully closed material is material that is non-accessible and/or non-reusable. Although this may stem from intellectual property rights, and by extension a licence or a lack thereof, it is more likely that fully closed status will arise through non-intellectual restrictions. These may include an item that has heavily deteriorated to the point at which access would be liable to damage or destroy it disproportionately. Fully closed status may arise in connection with intellectual property rights, the most obvious example being where a rights holder fails to issue any licences in relation to their work. Nevertheless, that work will only be fully closed if the rights holder also maintains control over the recorded or encoded information, since once the work or a copy of it is materially available to others the information will be accessible and, under exceptions to copyright, in some cases reusable.

Semi-closed material

The status of being semi-closed is more significant and more likely to arise in connection with intellectual property and the digitised collections of cultural heritage organisations. Semi-closed material, while at times valid and necessary, also presents the greatest danger of materials being unnecessarily restricted. Material is semi-closed when it falls between being fully closed and open. This is a wide scale, and encompasses everything from material that is subject to restrictive, exclusive licence arrangements to material that is widely available under a more restrictive form of 'open' licence (that nevertheless does not meet that 'openness' threshold).

Notably, at the more open end of the semi-closed scale is material that has been made available under a minimally restrictive licence, such as a Creative Commons licence with a non-commercial or no-derivatives element. For example, a work available under the Creative Commons Attribution NonCommercial ShareAlike (CC BY-NC-SA) licence is semi-closed, albeit far towards the 'open' end of that scale. The licensed material is not properly 'open', because, while it may (from a licensing perspective) be accessed, used, modified and shared (subject to maintaining provenance through attribution), no such activities may occur that are commercial in nature. If a party other than the copyright owner wishes to modify the material for a commercial purpose, for example to create a textbook, they need to obtain separate permission from the copyright owner. Clearly, CC BY-NC-SA licensed material is more 'open' than restrictively and exclusively licensed material, which may, for example, prevent use by all but a sole party; it nevertheless falls short of being truly open, thus misses out on some of the key benefits and opportunities of openness. Figure 4.1 illustrates open, semi-closed and closed licences.

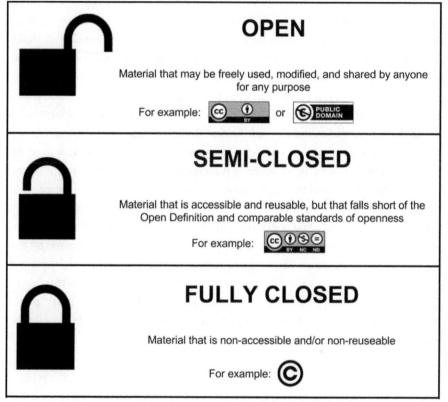

Figure 4.1   *Definitions of open, semi-closed and closed resources (CC BY)*
Source: Gill Hamilton, Fred Saunderson, Creative Commons

Reasons for maintaining closed material

It may at times be valid and correct, even necessary, to maintain material in cultural and information institutions that is 'closed'. It is essential that a semi-closed status is not maintained as a default, however, or without due consideration. Reversion to closed status by default can be easily done if insufficient consideration is given to desired outcomes and intentions or without identification of digital *raison d'être*. The reasons for closing content should be specific, identified and isolated. Furthermore, the mechanisms by which closed status is maintained (e.g. the type of licence used) should be considered, specific and sustainable. Proper use of licences and rights statements, albeit more restrictive when used with open content, can be an important tool.

Material that is protected by third party intellectual property rights is the most obvious, and likely most common, reason for maintaining closed material. If an organisation is granted permission by a copyright owner to digitise and make material available, it is likely and entirely correct that the organisation may be asked that reuse restrictions are in place if the content is made available to users. In such cases, the institution has an obligation to protect the rights of the third party, and there will be a justifiable balance between the degree of access and usability that is afforded and the level of rights retention that the third party maintains.

Another instance where semi-closed status may be justified is where an organisation has created digitisations of material in the public domain, but where a third party has funded the digitisation or otherwise provided assistance. In a case like this, where the institution would be unable to make the material digitally available without external resources, there is justification for a degree of restriction to be placed on the derived copies of the material if so desired by the funding or assisting party. However, it is crucial that the institution does not assume restriction or restrict material as a default. It would not be justifiable to restrict material on third party assistance grounds if the third party never expressed a desire for restriction or was willing to provide comparable assistance without it.

Notes

1   Enumerate, Digitisation Activity in Europe's Cultural Heritage Institutions, 2014, www.enumerate.eu/en/statistics/.

2   Tanner, S., Open GLAM: the rewards (and some risks) of digital sharing for the public good. In Wallace, A. and Deazley, R. (eds), *Display At Your Own Risk*, 2016, http://displayatyourownrisk.org/tanner/.

3   Neely, L., Creating Culture By, With and For the Public. In Wallace, A. and Deazley, R. (eds), *Display At Your Own Risk*, 2016, http://displayatyourownrisk.org/neely/.

4   See, for example, Roasati, E., Originality in a Work, or a Work of Originality: the effects of the Infopaq decision, *European Intellectual Property Review*, **33** (12), 2011, 746–55, hdl.handle.net/1814/20561; Savvides, T. and Ibbetson, S., Brexit and Copyright Law: will the English courts revert to the 'old' test for originality?, Kluwer Copyright Blog, 5 December 2016, http://kluwercopyrightblog.com/2016/12/05/brexit-copyright-law-will-english-courts-revert-old-test-originality/; Derclaye (18) cites a raft of post-Infopaq UK Court of Appeal case law as 'very unsettled' over the matter or originality: Derclaye, E., Assessing the Impact and Reception of the Court of Justice of the European Union Case Law on UK copyright law: what does the future hold?, *Revue Internationale du Droit d'Auteur*, 2014, 5–117, eprints.nottingham.ac.uk/3613/.

5   Alexa, How Popular is Wikipedia.org?, 2017, www.alexa.com/siteinfo/wikipedia.org.

6   Alexa, How Popular is Metmuseum.org, 2017, www.alexa.com/siteinfo/metmuseum.org; Alexa, How Popular is bl.uk?, 2017, www.alexa.com/siteinfo/bl.uk; Alexa, How Popular is rijksmuseum.nl?, 2017, www.alexa.com/siteinfo/rijksmuseum.nl.

7   Wikipedia, Wikipedia:Non-free content, 2017, https://en.wikipedia.org/wiki/Wikipedia:Non-free_content.

8   Wikimedia Tool Labs, BaGLAMa 2: category details for collections of the National Library Wales, 2017, tools.wmflabs.org/glamtools/baglama2/#gid=162&month=201607.

9   Stein, R., Museums . . . so what?, Code | Words: technology and theory in the museum, 4 June 2014, https://medium.com/code-words-technology-and-theory-in-the-museum/museums-so-what-7b4594e72283.

10 Europeana, A Call to Culture: Europeana 2020 strategic update, n.d., http://strategy2020.europeana.eu/.

11 Enumerate, Digitisation Activity in Europe's Cultural Heritage Institutions.

12 Rodley, E., *The Virtues of Promiscuity: or, why giving it away is the future*, Code | Words: Technology and Theory in the Museum, 7 July 2014, https://medium.com/code-words-technology-and-theory-in-the-museum/ the-virtues-of-promiscuity-cb89342ca038.

13 IBM News Room, IBM 2010 Global CEO Study: creativity selected as most crucial factor for future success, news release, 18 May 2010, https://www-03.ibm.com/press/us/en/pressrelease/31670.wss.

14 Enumerate, Digitisation Activity in Europe's Cultural Heritage Institutions.

15 Crews, K. D., Museum Policies and Art Images: conflicting objectives and

copyright overreaching, *Fordham Intellectual Property, Media & Entertainment Law Journal*, **22**, 2012, 795, ssrn.com/abstract=2120210.

16 Siegal, N., Masterworks for One and All, *The New York Times*, 28 May 2013, www.nytimes.com/2013/05/29/arts/design/museums-mull-public-use-of-online-art-images.html.

17 Intellectual Property Office, How Do @NPGLondon Manage the #Copyright of 'National Treasures' like Shakespeare?, 10 July 2016, https://twitter.com/The_IPO/status/752094523065454592; Anthony, D., National Treasures, Intellectual Property Office blog, https://ipo.blog.gov.uk/2016/07/07/national-treasures/.

18 Pekel, J., Democratising the Rijksmuseum: why did the Rijksmuseum make available their highest quality material without restrictions, and what are the results?, Europeana Professional, 2014, http://pro.europeana.eu/files/Europeana_Professional/Publications/Democratising%20the%20Rijksmuseum.pdf.

19 Enumerate, Digitisation Activity in Europe's Cultural Heritage Institutions.

20 Kelly, K., *Images of Works of Art in Museum Collections: the experience of open access, a study of 11 museums*, Council on Library and Information Resources, 2013, www.clir.org/pubs/reports/pub157/pub157.pdf.

21 Benjamin, W., The Work of Art in the Age of Mechanical Reproduction, Marxists Internet Archive, 1936, www.marxists.org/reference/subject/philosophy/works/ge/benjamin.htm.

22 Siegal, N., Masterworks for One and All, *The New York Times*, 28 May 2013, www.nytimes.com/2013/05/29/arts/design/museums-mull-public-use-of-online-art-images.html.

23 Open Definition, Open Definition 2.1, n.d., http://opendefinition.org/od/2.1/en/.

Introduction to case studies

So far, this book has explored the fundamentals of openness and licensing. We have looked at the provenance of the open movement and the realities of the current copyright environment. We have also advanced our arguments for why cultural heritage organisations should adopt an open approach. Before this book turns to the practical details of implementing open licences and using openly licensed material, we will look at a number of contributed case studies.

A range of organisations have undertaken efforts to adopt open approaches. These organisations, from public libraries to national museums, have used open licences to help make openness a viable reality in fields and disciplines as diverse as education, data, art and metadata. This section of the book explores how seven cultural and information organisations – Statens Museum for Kunst (National Gallery of Denmark), the National Library of Wales, the British Library, Newcastle Libraries, the National Library of Scotland, the Wellcome Library and the University of Edinburgh – have developed their approaches to being open and by using open licences have moulded, aided and stabilised these efforts.

These case studies have been contributed by experts and practitioners working within these organisations. Each study brings a distinct voice and experience, and each focuses on a particular aspect of openness and licensing.

We have provided these diverse case studies with the aim of rooting the concept of open licensing in real world experience. We hope that these examples – drawn from distinct fields, varied regions and organisations large and small – will enable practitioners in cultural heritage to further explore the benefits and realities of openness in practice and to gain valuable insight into the steps that others have taken and the lessons learned from early adopters.

Chapter 5

Small steps, big impact: how SMK became SMK Open

Merete Sanderhoff

Starting small

> Think Big. Start Small. Move Fast.   (Michael Edson)

This simple piece of advice has been a key driving factor to achieve the ambition of opening up the digitised collection of Statens Museum for Kunst (National Gallery of Denmark; SMK). The advice was given to us in 2011 by Michael Edson, then Director of Web and New Media Strategy at The Smithsonian Institution. At the time, we were in the midst of a process discussing and reconsidering the image licensing policy for our online collection. Like so many other cultural heritage institutions around the world, we had extended our policy from the analogue era into the digital age. We were still charging licensing and transaction fees for use of digital images, even though, in principle, reproductions of artworks in our collection could now be distributed with zero marginal cost. And even though, in reality, most of our collection is in the public domain because of its age and therefore rightly belongs to the public. In the 'forever business' of cultural heritage, business as usual has a tendency to prevail.

At that particular moment, SMK had been contacted by Google staff. They wanted SMK to join their Art Project, which in its first launch had sported such notable museum collections as the Gemäldegalerie in Berlin, the Uffizi in Florence, and the Metropolitan Museum of Art in New York. It was one of those offers you cannot refuse. The invitation spurred some significant internal debates at SMK. We had been following the news of museums releasing their digitised collections using Creative Commons – from Rijksmuseum to Yale University. The digital team had been making the argument about open data, pointing to the potential of the Creative Commons system for our collection, and for a while we had internal discussions of pros and cons. But the call from Google proved to be the tipping point.

SMK is a publicly funded art museum. Google is a private company. If SMK were to join the Google Art Project, it would enter into a so-called public–private partnership, effectively handing over usage rights to digitised cultural heritage that is collectively owned and funded by the citizens of Denmark. In their contract, Google conditioned that they would gain full usage rights to the high-resolution images of artworks donated by SMK to the Art Project, images for which SMK would normally charge a licensing fee.

On the one hand, we could see enormous potential in showcasing the SMK collection on Google's powerful platform. On the other, we realised that if we were to give away the use rights to high quality image files for free to a private company, it would be ethically wrong to keep charging money for those same image files from the public who initially funded their digitisation via taxes. If we were going to give them to Google, we had to also give them to everyone. So that is what we did.

With this shift, we wanted to change the capacity of our collection from a passive to an active asset. While we cannot allow people to touch the original artworks because of the potential risk of damaging them, once they are digitised people can touch, sample, repurpose and remix them without breaking the originals. In this way, we could hand over the collection that we steward, and which is in fact the property of the public, to the people and let them use it as a toolbox – an active resource at the tips of their fingers.

This may sound like a bold move. But we started with just a tiny fraction of our collection. From a collection of 260,000 objects spanning 700 years of art from medieval times to the present, we selected just 160 highlights that are completely free of copyright because of their age, and which we therefore could share with Google, and with everyone, without any restrictions. This is where Michael Edson's advice came in: 160 high-resolution images, with clean metadata as well as textual and video interpretation in two languages, was all we had resources to prepare for Google Art Project – and hence for release to the general public – at the time. When looking out on the landscape of international museums opening up their collections in tens or hundreds of thousands of objects at a time, our contribution felt embarrassingly small. But Edson gave us the advice to start with just those 160 images and make a big celebration of their radical reuse potentials. This involved putting them on as many external platforms as possible – from Google Art to Pinterest, Flickr and Wikimedia Commons – and actively supporting interested communities in using them for their own purposes.

Choosing the right licence

In order to hand over use rights to the museum's official reproductions of the collection we applied a licence from the Creative Commons package to them. Creative Commons is a flexible system that aims to support the diversity of creators' wishes and needs when publishing their work in an age of easy, instant sharing and distribution. But for that reason it is also less simple than the all-rights-reserved copyright scheme (in-copyright, or not in-copyright). It is a buffet of options, which can be combined in a multitude of ways.

Plunging into Creative Commons licensing for the first time gave rise to internal debates about which licence to opt for. It was important for us to include all internal stakeholders in the decision-making process, from curators and photographers to financial directors and digital producers. This led to valuable discussions, for instance about whether the original idea of an artwork is inviolable even after copyright has expired, whether it is within the scope of the mission of a publicly funded art museum to support commercial reuse of out-of-copyright collections, do freely reusable collections offer new potential to reach non-user segments of the population, and more. In the process, we considered almost every combination in the Creative Commons package, from the most restrictive (Attribution, NonCommercial and NoDerivatives) to the more liberal options like Attribution ShareAlike.

What helped us reach a decision was to scrutinise the licensing policies of other cultural heritage institutions pioneering the OpenGLAM movement (https://openglam.org/), which promotes free and open access to digital cultural heritage held by galleries, libraries, archives and museums (GLAMs). Champions of openness like the Rijksmuseum in Amsterdam and the National Gallery of Art in Washington DC were sharing their considerations and experiences in blogs and conferences, and it was helpful to study what these museums had done and what the outcomes were. Through their examples, we learned for instance about the huge potential in sharing museum collections on Wikimedia Commons where they would be used to illustrate thousands of Wikipedia articles in multiple languages, resulting in unprecedented global reach. This, however, required applying a liberal Creative Commons licence that would allow commercial and derivative reuse, because Wikipedia is an open encyclopedia, drawing only on truly open and reusable content from volunteer contributors all over the world. This became a crucial factor for our final decision about licensing.

And yet, the decision was not final after all. We knew we were trying out the Creative Commons system on a small sample of our collection to harvest experience and feedback from creative and cultural heritage communities, and the general public. We were keenly aware that applying a Creative Commons licence to artworks that are lawfully in the public domain because of their age is actually a violation of the whole idea of the public domain as a commons – a piece of shared property which we all have innate rights to use. Europeana is the main platform for Europe's digitised cultural heritage, and in its public domain charter it is clearly stated, 'Works that are in the Public Domain in analogue form continue to be in the Public Domain once they have been digitised.'[1]

All of the Creative Commons licences, ranging from the prohibitive CC BY-NC-NC to the liberal CC BY, add a new layer of restriction to images of artworks in the public domain. However, pragmatically, going from all rights reserved to some rights reserved significantly enhances users' rights to reuse a creative work. Being a research-based institution, it felt important to many employees at SMK to insist on proper attribution in order to protect the original sources of the digital reproductions. At the same time, there was consensus that our images should be fit for reuse in Wikipedia and on social media, to reap the benefits of having our collection exposed and freely shared on platforms that reach many more people than will ever visit SMK's own website. For our pilot project of releasing 160 highlights, we opted for the most liberal of the Creative Commons licences, CC BY, which allows any kind of reuse, including for commercial purposes and derivative works, as long as the source is properly credited.

Open access is just the first step

In April 2012 we proudly launched our first batch of high quality images for free download under CC BY 3.0 on our website. The images were provided in JPEG format, in the highest quality available ranging in size from 10 MB to 500 MB. All preparatory work for the release had been carried out manually as we did not have an infrastructure in place to connect high-resolution images in our image repository with metadata in our database, textual interpretation in our content management system, and videos on our YouTube channel. Our existing website was not geared towards self-service download, so our IT manager had to set up a separate server to enable this new functionality. The user interface was not designed for the purpose. We had to make do with what our content management system could muster – which resulted in making the images available for batch download in three separate zip files, and individually in a seemingly endless scroll. Not the most elegant solution, but we kept in mind that we were starting small.

The amazing thing is that the reaction to our humble open collection was overwhelming. The news was shared widely across social media and referenced in blogs, and soon we were seeing creative reuse, from digital remixes to artworks displayed on high definition home TVs and paintings printed on pillow cases. Within no time, Wikimedians had uploaded the images to Wikimedia Commons and started using them to illustrate Wikipedia articles. The impact was impressive, even with such a small sample of our collection. The images were soon featured in several hundred articles in 27 different languages.

In a case study issued by Creative Commons, a member of the Wikimedia community commented on the release of the 160 SMK highlights:

> When SMK releases images of 160 artworks under CC BY, it means that we in Wikipedia (as well as the other Wikimedia projects) are able to write better articles about both the artists, the artworks, and the motifs. One example: In 1646, Jan van Goyen painted a prospect of the city of Arnhem. This image is not only fit to illustrate the article about van Goyen, but also the one about Arnhem, 1646, tonal landscape painting, and tulipomania – not just in Danish, but in all the languages that Wikipedia is available in. Furthermore, images and texts can be reused elsewhere on the Internet to the benefit of many more users.[2]

Figure 5.1   *Jan van Goyen (1596–1656), View of the City of Arnhem, 1646, KMS317* [3]
Source: Statens Museum for Kunst (http://collection.smk.dk/#/en/detail/KMS317)

Following the advice of Michael Edson and the example of other OpenGLAM museums we did not just sit back and wait for people to start doing stuff with our collections. We actively reached out to communities of creatives and learners, encouraging them to reuse our images, and celebrating their efforts on SMK's official platforms. We quickly established new partnerships with artists, designers, bloggers, school teachers and students for whom freely available, high quality images from a trusted source were a valuable asset.

One project worth highlighting is Cool Constructions, a collaboration between the Art Pilots – SMK's volunteer task force of young creatives – the Copenhagen Metro Company and local residents living by metro construction sites.⁴ The Copenhagen metro is being expanded significantly towards 2023, and many locals are inconvenienced in the process. A characteristic feature of the ongoing metro construction is the long green fences shielding off construction sites all over town. The Metro Company has turned those fences into urban canvases where alternating creative projects unfold. In 2013, SMK facilitated a project where the Art Pilots helped local residents develop a huge decoration for their metro fence, based on open SMK images (Figure 5.2). The Art Pilots ran a series of workshops with the locals where they worked together on remixing

Figure 5.2   *Art Pilots mounting the Metro fence in central Copenhagen, 2013, photo CC BY 3.0*
Source: Frida Gregersen

selected images into a highly imaginative digital collage using Photoshop. The result is a 70-metre long remix comprising artworks from the Renaissance to Realism that have been digitally twisted, tattooed and tagged in street art style.[5]

This fence – almost as a contradiction in terms – turned out to be a real breakthrough for SMK's open image policy. The Cool Construction remix received praise in the media and was awarded a prize as the most popular fence of the year 2013.[6] The local residents agreed; they have asked for the remix to remain on their fence for the entire construction period. Based on the great feedback of this small outreach project, we felt encouraged to introduce a museum-wide policy shift for our digitised collection.

Embracing the public domain

Trying out Creative Commons on a very limited sample of our collection was a deliberate way to test open licensing on a small scale we felt comfortable with. Once we had tangible evidence of the positive effects of open licensing, the first thing we did when moving from pilot to policy was to reopen the internal discussion on Creative Commons licences. As stated, we were keenly aware that adding a licence, however liberal, to artworks in the public domain was an infringement of the very idea of the public domain we were trying to celebrate. Therefore, when formulating the museum's overall open policy it was pivotal for us to fully acknowledge the public domain.

However, this ambition put us through a new process of legal clarification. In Danish copyright law, it is not possible simply to place reproductions of public domain artworks in the public domain using the Creative Commons public domain mark (which is not a licence, just a marker to state clearly that a work is out-of-copyright). All photographs are protected by copyright for 50 years from the moment the picture was taken, and the copyright is owned by the person who clicked the button. In our case, even though SMK was ready to hand over our images to the public domain, the copyright of our photographers stood in the way. However, after careful scrutiny of previous legal cases and court rulings, we found out that any production made within work hours by permanent staff of a public institution, which can be deemed to be part of normal tasks for the staff, by default accrues to the employer. Still, the photographic copyright had to be waived, which was possible using the Creative Commons Public Domain Dedication, commonly known as CC Zero (CC0).

You might wonder why it was so important for us to shift from CC BY to CC0. In practice, the two allow precisely the same liberties to the user, with the only exception that CC BY demands attribution. However, in the pilot period we neither had the intention, nor the resources, to check if every use of our open images was properly attributed. So the difference is of principle rather than practical in nature. With CC BY you claim that you own the copyright, but you are willing to share use rights on specific conditions. With CC0 you tell the public: this belongs to you, you are free to use it for anything you like, no strings attached.

For generations, we have been brought up to think of cultural heritage as untouchable, distant, behind armoured glass and alarm systems that prevent the public from coming too close to the art. With digitisation, this condition is fundamentally changed. Once an artwork is digitised, we can share it in endless numbers of copies at zero marginal cost, and people can play and remix and share it all they want without damaging the original. We need to reprogramme our minds to think of museums as places where all citizens of society are equally entitled to be, and of our collections as something we take care of on behalf of the public who rightfully owns them.

Sharing digital copies without restrictions poses a highly effective way to turn what formerly could only be enjoyed passively from a distance into active tools in the hands of users. On top of that, we can bring our collection to the farthest corners of society, where people who would never in their life have a chance to pass the threshold of the museum in Copenhagen can get up close and personal with our masterpieces. Open collections open up entirely new perspectives for social impact.

To me, one of the most powerful examples so far of the social potential of our open collection was created in 2015, when the Art Pilots did a remix project in collaboration with the users of a drug injection room in central Copenhagen called Skyen ('The Cloud') (Figure 5.3 opposite). The idea was to enhance the atmosphere in this rather impersonal clinical space, using digitised artworks from SMK's open collections, to turn it into a place that represents the ideas and dreams of its users. In the process, the Art Pilots and the users of Skyen worked together to select appealing images and motifs and remix them digitally. The result is a drug injection room radically transformed from a sterile, anonymous space into a room imbued with the personal stories and aspirations of its users (Figure 5.4). It is a place they feel proud of, because it represents their unique identities, not labelling them as social outcasts but as human beings like you and me who have creative ideas, dreams and complex life stories to tell.

Turning our art collection into an open toolbox that can spur the imagination of people who are not likely to visit the museum, or do not have a strong

Figure 5.3   *Art Pilots remaking the injection room Skyen in Copenhagen, 2015, CC BY 4.0*
Source: Unges Laboratorier for Kunst

Figure 5.4   *The injection room Skyen after the makeover, 2015, CC BY 4.0*
Source: Unges Laboratorier for Kunst

relationship with old master paintings, offering them a chance to connect with their beauty, serenity and stories in ways that make sense to them – all of this is only possible because we have let go of control over how these artworks may be used. This bold concept developed by the Art Pilots underlines how when opened up for new creative usages, museum collections can become tools that have social impact in real people's lives, outside the museum walls.

Collaborating around an open collection

With the official announcement of our public domain policy in 2015, we launched all of our online collection of 25,000 images for free download. In a blog post leading up to the launch, the director of SMK Mikkel Bogh formulated the mindset behind our open collection:

> With our digitized collection we can help educate and enlighten people, supporting them in their endeavours to become reflecting, creative individuals. But in order for this to happen our cultural heritage must belong to everyone, and each of us must be free to use it in exactly the ways we need and dream of. As museums, we do not hold any patent on how cultural heritage can and should be interpreted and used. Our role is increasingly to facilitate the general public's use of cultural heritage for learning, creativity and innovation. Today, the museum as a place of enlightenment is based on interaction. We are all part of this web. We enlighten each other.[7]

With this statement, the museum assumes a new role as facilitator of other people's learning, creativity and enjoyment of the arts, on *their* terms. At the same time, museum professionals take an open position to learn about our collections from the ways the public interacts with it.

In the wake of our policy shift, an important strategic area of action is to build a strong partnership with Wikipedia. This platform is an essential hub today for anyone seeking knowledge and source materials on just about any topic in the universe. For more than three years we have been running monthly Wiki Labs at SMK, in collaboration with colleague museums also working with open collections. The idea is to bring together Wikipedians, museum professionals and art enthusiasts to learn about Wikipedia editing and be able to write better, more accurate Wikipedia entries on art historical topics, to enhance, as it were, the online source where most people begin their research, by equipping it with valid reproductions of original artworks and consistent links to trusted sources.

The impact we can achieve through Wikipedia is evident. Open images from SMK led to around 20 million page views on Wikipedia in 2015. In 2016, this number had risen to 33 million. In comparison, during the same year we had a total of about 770,000 sessions on our own domain smk.dk. And we reached 3.7 million on our Facebook page, our largest social media platform. Page views on Wikipedia are obviously not equal to deep engagement. But it is an indicator of the enormous potential there of reaching out and meeting new users of our collection. It is a lot of work to build and manage the Wiki Labs community and ensure that it continues to thrive, and it requires a huge concerted effort to enhance just a small corner of the collective art historical material represented in Wikipedia. But it is worth the effort, and the more people who contribute, the farther we can get. Figure 5.5 shows the reach of SMK content on several online platforms in 2016.

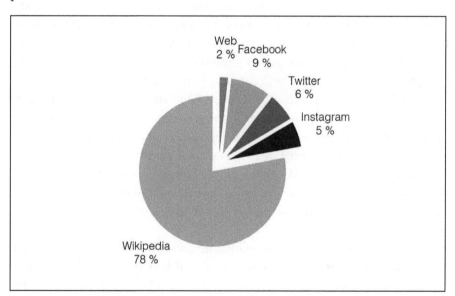

Figure 5.5   *Pie chart showing the reach of SMK content on various online platforms in 2016, Jonas Heide Smith*
Source: Statens Museum for Kunst

Running Wiki Labs as a dynamic community that stays in touch between monthly meetups via a dedicated Facebook group has proven to be a viable strategy. Within the last year, we have grown to a community of almost 150 people, both amateurs and professionals, from all over Denmark, and the hosting of Wiki Labs is now shared by three institutions in Copenhagen, with plans to reach out to more partners in the coming year.

What is the impact of having an open approach?

Having worked with open collections for a couple of years now, we have come to an important realisation: capturing the reuse of our images and data, not to mention the wider societal impact of increased access to cultural heritage which we aim to achieve, is a hard nut to crack. How can we provide real evidence that we are reaching our objectives, beyond the anecdotal and the circumstantial?

The digitisation of cultural heritage collections promises unprecedented potential for the GLAM sector to fulfil its public mission of opening up knowledge and culture to the participation and enjoyment of all citizens. Open culture has been claimed to increase our sense of collective identity, fuel new creative entrepreneurship, and play a crucial role in education and lifelong learning. How can we demonstrate that we are consistently achieving this ambition?

Increasingly, our sector is under pressure. Politicians and funders are demanding numbers to show that the tax or private money spent on culture have tangible social impact: how have peoples' opportunities to learn, create and contribute to their culture and society improved after we started providing access to digitised collections? Is it worth continued investment?

In 2016, with the support of the Danish foundation Nordea-fonden, SMK embarked on a four year project to open up our digitised collections at scale. The project SMK Open revolves around building a solid infrastructure that will allow both the museum and external users to access and reuse our collection data and content easily and flexibly. SMK Open provides a great opportunity to conduct the first strategic and comprehensive study in the history of SMK of the wider socio-cultural impact of opening up and facilitating reuse of a public domain art collection.

Over the last few years, Europeana has invested great effort in developing a framework to assess the impact digitised cultural heritage can have on society, economy and innovation when openly shared. The first iteration of the Europeana Impact Assessment Framework (IAF) was launched in autumn 2016. At the outset of 2017, in partnership with Europeana, we are using SMK Open as a case study for impact assessment, to further develop and refine the IAF prototype, and to gather tangible evidence about the socio-cultural effects of having turned our collection into a free and open toolbox for the citizens of the world. Our shared ambition is to develop a validated set of tools that will be useful to cultural institutions everywhere in capturing the value of opening up their collections so people can create culture, not just look at it.

Based on our experience so far, we have a good case for the potentials of open cultural heritage. But our partnership with Europeana is challenging us to think differently about what kind of role we can play in a world fuelled by digital technologies. Can museums support people in acquiring new skills, exploring their own creativity, experiencing the act of learning as something compelling and fun? Could we even empower citizens to feel more included in culture, in democracy, in society? Impact assessment might not only enable us to assess that open is good, but help us understand better what we can do to maximise the impact our museum – and museums everywhere – can have in society, and in people's lives.

Notes

1   Europeana, 'Public domain charter', n.d.,
www.europeana.eu/portal/en/rights/public-domain-charter.html.
2   Creative Commons Wiki, Case Studies/Highlights from SMK, The National Gallery of Denmark, 2012,
wiki.creativecommons.org/wiki/Case_Studies/Highlights_from_SMK,_ The_National_Gallery_of_Denmark.
3   National Gallery of Denmark, Jan van Goyen (1596–1656), View of the City of Arnhem, 2017, www.smk.dk/en/explore-the-art/highlights/jan-van-goyen-view-of-the-city-of-arnhem/.
4   Copenhagen Metro, Cool Construction, n.d.,
http://intl.m.dk/about+the+metro/metro+expansion/cool+construction.
5   For example, see newspaper coverage: Hornung, P. M., Guldalder og galskab på gadeplan, *PressReader*, 16 August 2013,
www.pressreader.com/denmark/politiken/20130816/281560878438013.
6   Københavns Metro, Hegnspælen 2013, 2013,
www.m.dk/#!/om+metroen/metrobyggeriet/byens+hegn/hegnspaelen+2013.
7   National Gallery of Denmark, Mikkel Bogh Blogs: enlightenment in the age of digitisation, blog, 10 September 2014, www.smk.dk/en/explore-the-art/smk-blogs/artikel/mikkel-bogh-blogs-enlightenment-in-the-age-of-digitisation/.

References

Europeana Professional, The Europeana Public Domain Charter, 2010,
http://pro.europeana.eu/publication/the-europeana-public-domain-charter.
Fallon, J. and Verwayen, H., A Fresh Perspective on Exploring Impact, Europeana Professional, 25 November 2016, pro.europeana.eu/blogpost/ a-fresh-perspective-on-exploring-impact.

National Gallery of Denmark, SMK Open, 2016,
    www.smk.dk/en/about-smk/camp00/.
National Gallery of Denmark, Digital Casts, n.d.,
    www.smk.dk/en/visit-the-museum/smk2/digital-casts-of-sculptures/.
Smithsonian Institution, Web and New Media Strategy: version 1.0, 30 July 2009,
    www.si.edu/Content/Pdf/About/Web-New-Media-Strategy_v1.0.pdf.
Wiki Labs – enriching art history on Wikipedia, Statens Museum for Kunst, 2015,
    www.smk.dk/en/explore-the-art/smk-blogs/artikel/translate-to-english-wiki-labs-
    berigelse-af-kunsthistorien-paa-wikipedia/.
Wikimedia Commons, Images Released Under the CC0 1.0 Universal License by
    Statens Museum for Kunst, 2015,
    www.commons.wikimedia.org/wiki/Category:Images_released_under_
    the_CC0_1.0_Universal_license_by_Statens_Museum_for_Kunst.

Chapter 6

The British Library experience of open metadata licensing

Neil Wilson, Head of Collection Metadata, The British Library

The British Library and open bibliographic metadata

The British Library is the national library of the UK. Among its core responsibilities set out in the British Library Act 1972 is that of disseminating metadata describing its rich collections and UK publishing output since 1950 via the British National Bibliography (www.bl.uk/bibliographic/natbib.html). This requirement resulted in the Library offering bibliographic metadata services from its foundation. These services were originally operated commercially and were primarily aimed solely at the library community. However, in 2010 the British Library began to develop an open metadata strategy in response to calls from the UK government, such as *Putting the Frontline First*, which encouraged increased access to public sector data in order to promote transparency, economic growth and research.[1] At the same time there was growing interest in the potential of linked data for improving reach to new users and exploiting new information sources. Such opportunities were felt compelling enough to warrant action despite the significant technical and licensing issues that needed to be addressed.

The new open metadata strategy aimed to remove constraints imposed by restrictive licensing and domain specific library standards (e.g. MARC21) and to develop new modes of access with communities using the metadata. It was believed that proactively enabling the reuse of metadata could increase its community value, improve access to information and culture, while reinforcing the relevance of libraries. However, in order to justify and sustain the initiative in a period of diminishing funding it was important to try to achieve institutional recognition via any licence model selected to support reuse. In addition, a number of risks required active management, notably:

- legal risks, for example complex copyright and licensing frameworks that require proactive management of derived metadata licensing to protect against possible liabilities
- reputational risks, for example possible perception that the British Library is not satisfying government and community expectations due to variant definitions of 'open' data.

Rather than create a targeted service that satisfied only one audience segment or a generic offering that risked satisfying none, a multi-track approach was adopted to address the requirements of three core user groups: researchers, linked data users and developers, and libraries.

Access, standards and licence options were then tailored to the specific needs of these groups.

Licence choices

In order to mitigate the risks noted above, research was undertaken on the open licensing options available together with any implications for the metadata services to be offered. An initial concern was the variation in interpretation of the terms 'free' and 'open' data in online community discussions (Figure 6.1).

Free data	Open data
Of cost?	To access from anywhere?
Of all licensing restrictions?	To modify or enhance?
To sell or reuse in commercial services?	To use with free software?
To copy and redistribute?	To link from your data or system?

Figure 6.1   *Interpretation of the terms 'free' and 'open' data in online community discussions*

On examination of the activities of other organisations it also became apparent that few institutions offered completely unconditional, perpetual access to their data and normally parameterised open datasets in accordance with recognised organisational restrictions (Figure 6.2 opposite).

Organisational restrictions	Organisational defined parameters of open data	
	Scope	Permissions
Ownership and licensing agreements Legislation (e.g. the Data Protection Act) Technical issues (e.g. data non-standard, non-open format) Institutional policy on sharing with for-profit organisations, etc. Funding agencies, policies	Data format Coverage and inclusions policy Delivery routes (e.g. web, ftp) Level of user support (if any)	To use for any purpose forever To study and adapt for local use To redistribute copies To improve and release to the community

Figure 6.2   *Typical organisational restrictions and defined parameters of open data*

Since the British Library had originally licensed derived, third party metadata with a view to commercial re-supply via its priced bibliographic services, it was also in the fortunate position of being able to offer such metadata free of charge. However, while British Library agreements with third party metadata suppliers allowed free supply of MARC records, some accommodation was necessary. Such measures were required to prevent suppliers being put out of business by the British Library offering their MARC data without charge. Fortunately, the fact that MARC21 is not recognised as an open data format assisted with this issue since user feedback and government best practice suggested that XML and linked data serialisation formats, such as RDF (Resource Description Framework), were more appropriate solutions. It was thus possible to come up with options for creating open data that met wider community expectations without a negative effect on third parties. Discussions also indicated that some commercial suppliers were even willing to allow the Library to offer selective MARC record supply services (e.g. ISBN Search) under open licences as long as they did not allow complete datasets to be resupplied.

Another issue requiring investigation related to the question of how the intellectual property rights and copyright of a bibliographic record might be categorised given that some of its components – title, author's name, ISBN and so on – were not actually created by the cataloguing agency. The approach adopted in consultation with licensing experts was to treat bibliographic records as 'created works', assembled from a combination of information in the public domain together with institutionally generated data elements.

Licence selection was further complicated by the British Library's status as a public sector organisation and the need to review the implications of licence jurisdiction, UK government licensing practice and Crown copyright. Similarly, the relevance of data specific licensing terms, such as the Open Data Commons Open Database Licence, required examination.

Ultimately, although investigations identified over 70 potential licence permutations for putting data into the public domain while offering attribution and protection against possible liabilities, it was felt that the option offering the best balance of flexibility, protection and potential for attribution was Creative Commons Zero 1.0 Universal (CC0 1.0) Public Domain Dedication with voluntary attribution.[2]

This was the reasoning behind this choice:

- Government licences were not appropriate as the metadata being offered was copyright to the British Library Board rather than the Crown because of the organisation's quasi-autonomous non-governmental organisation (QUANGO) status.
- While data specific licences such as the Open Database Licence included useful features, they were generally designed around defined datasets for which some degree of intellectual property rights might be claimed. However the open metadata strategy aimed to offer users an opportunity to define their own, unique selections of database records for reuse in new composite datasets. Thus it was felt that a more flexible licensing option would be appropriate.
- Feedback on a pilot open data release offered under a Creative Commons Attribution NonCommercial (CC BY-NC) option was somewhat negative as users felt unable to reuse metadata with other more permissively licensed data to create their own CC0 datasets or services.
- CC0 offered the Library's metadata in the most permissive way for all user types including those wishing to reuse metadata in commercial services and thus it fitted well with the UK government's goal of stimulating economic growth as well as the Library's own objective of assisting research.

Outcomes

After consultation with potential users, it was decided that the multi-track approach to open library metadata would be best supported by service options based around a default CC0 position (Table 6.1 opposite).

As libraries were potentially large consumers of open bibliographic data but unlikely to possess systems capable of processing open data formats, like RDF, it was important to identify suitable technical and licensing options for their needs.

Table 6.1   *Service options for British Library user groups, by licence, format and access route*

User group	Licence	Formats	Access route
Researchers	CC0	CSV, RDF/XML	Bulk data dump via non-authenticated FTP
Linked data users and developers	CC0	RDF XML, RDF triples, JSON, TTL, HTML	Non-authenticated SPARQL; endpoint and non-authenticated FTP data dump
Libraries	British Library terms	MARC 21	Authenticated ANSI Z39.50 for selective item searching (e.g. ISBN)

The solution adopted was to offer free metadata via a library standard, search and retrieve protocol (ANSI Z39.50) in a common MARC variant (MARC21). In order to receive a unique ID and password, reassure commercial MARC record suppliers and monitor possible abuse, users were requested to agree to a bespoke set of British Library licence terms.[3]

Registration was not pursued for CC0 services following some initial experimentation since feedback indicated it was perceived negatively by the open data community and even led to the circulation of outdated datasets via sharing sites. To ensure the official, current British Library open datasets were the first choice it was therefore agreed to make them available from the British Library website via unauthenticated FTP download with British Library CC0 licence documentation included in the .ZIP archive files.

Figure 6.3, page 116 and Figure 6.4, page 117, show the guidance the British Library provides on downloads and free data services on its Data Services web pages.

The British Library's adoption of a default CC0 stance for its open metadata led to a number of further internal measures to ensure the sustainability of this position, including:

- proactive licensing of new sources of derived metadata to support open services
- filtering of all metadata to be supplied to remove elements for which third party intellectual property rights might be claimed (e.g. abstracts, reviews) and ensure only descriptive elements were supplied

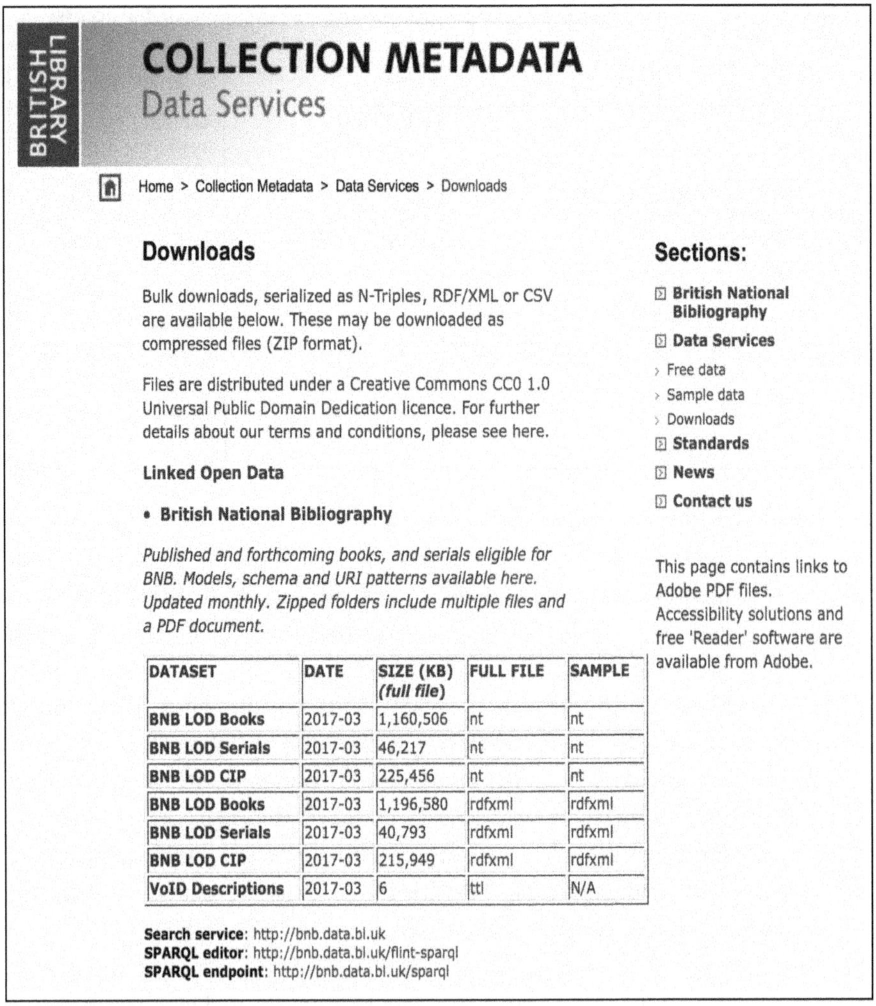

COLLECTION METADATA
Data Services

BRITISH LIBRARY

Home > Collection Metadata > Data Services > Downloads

Downloads

Bulk downloads, serialized as N-Triples, RDF/XML or CSV are available below. These may be downloaded as compressed files (ZIP format).

Files are distributed under a Creative Commons CC0 1.0 Universal Public Domain Dedication licence. For further details about our terms and conditions, please see here.

Linked Open Data

• **British National Bibliography**

Published and forthcoming books, and serials eligible for BNB. Models, schema and URI patterns available here. Updated monthly. Zipped folders include multiple files and a PDF document.

Sections:

▣ **British National Bibliography**

▣ **Data Services**
› Free data
› Sample data
› Downloads

▣ **Standards**

▣ **News**

▣ **Contact us**

This page contains links to Adobe PDF files. Accessibility solutions and free 'Reader' software are available from Adobe.

DATASET	DATE	SIZE (KB) (full file)	FULL FILE	SAMPLE
BNB LOD Books	2017-03	1,160,506	nt	nt
BNB LOD Serials	2017-03	46,217	nt	nt
BNB LOD CIP	2017-03	225,456	nt	nt
BNB LOD Books	2017-03	1,196,580	rdfxml	rdfxml
BNB LOD Serials	2017-03	40,793	rdfxml	rdfxml
BNB LOD CIP	2017-03	215,949	rdfxml	rdfxml
VoID Descriptions	2017-03	6	ttl	N/A

Search service: http://bnb.data.bl.uk
SPARQL editor: http://bnb.data.bl.uk/flint-sparql
SPARQL endpoint: http://bnb.data.bl.uk/sparql

Figure 6.3   *Download guidance on the British Library's Data Services web page*
Source: www.bl.uk/bibliographic/download.html ©The British Library Board, represented for the purposes for quotation

- negotiation of fixed embargo periods for metadata created for digitisation projects sponsored by commercial third parties to ensure that all data would ultimately be available for release
- differentiation between licensing terms negotiated for 'value added' metadata, such as book jackets, used to enhance the Library's public resource discovery systems and core descriptive 'inventory' metadata used to manage collections and to offer as part of open metadata services
- creation of a staff wiki centralising metadata licensing and best practice documentation

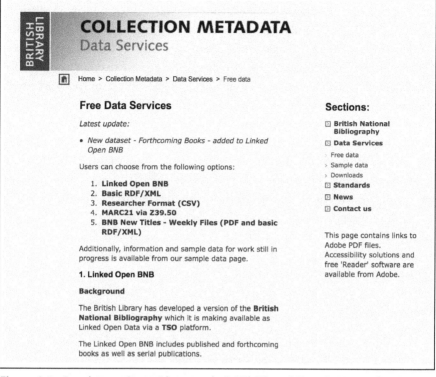

Figure 6.4   *Free data services guidance on the British Library's Data Services web page*
Source: www.bl.uk/bibliographic/datafree.html ©The British Library Board,
represented for the purposes for quotation

- inclusion of a commitment to open metadata services as a core priority of
  the British Library's first collection metadata strategy.[4]

Conclusions

The experience of investigating the detailed and interrelated legal, technical and
licensing issues surrounding open metadata was a steep learning curve for
library staff. However, it has ultimately proved beneficial in enabling the
development of sophisticated licensing strategies for both derived third party
metadata and open services. The knowledge gained has also proven valuable in
working with or advising other organisations developing their own open data
initiatives, such as The European Library's *English Short Title Catalogue*.

While the formats and systems used for the British Library's open metadata
have evolved in points of detail since 2010, user categories and related licence
options remain largely unchanged. Over 1680 organisations in 121 countries now
use the Library's open metadata services with many more taking single files. The

value of the British Library's open data work was recognised by the British National Bibliography linked dataset receiving a 5 star openness rating on the UK government Data.gov.uk site[5] and being certified by the Open Data Institute. This combination of recognition and usage helped to support the case for continued work on open data at a point when public sector resources were under considerable pressure from the economic downturn of 2008.

Such factors also helped to balance the challenges experienced in identifying service usage beyond raw figures for file downloads and linked data queries. Determining the impact of open data dumps has proven particularly difficult because of the general unwillingness of users of these CC0 services to register for access coupled with their minimal feedback. Ironically, this is in contrast to users taking the Library's authenticated Z39.50 service under more restrictive, non-commercial terms. Despite such challenges, the British Library remains committed to pursuing a CC0 approach to support the widest possible reuse of its metadata and thus generate the best return on the investment in its creation.

Notes

1   HM Treasury, *Putting the Frontline First: smarter government*, Cm 7753, 2009, www.gov.uk/government/uploads/system/uploads/attachment_data/file/228889/7753.pdf.

2   British Library, *British Library Catalogue Datasets in RDF and CSV*, n.d., www.bl.uk/bibliographic/pdfs/british_library_catalogue_dataset_tc.pdf.

3   British Library, Free Data Services: terms & conditions, n.d., www.bl.uk/bibliographic/dataterms.html.

4   British Library, *Unlocking The Value: the British Library's collection metadata strategy 2015–2018*, n.d., www.bl.uk/bibliographic/pdfs/british-library-collection-metadata-strategy-2015-2018.pdf.

5   Data.gov.uk, The Linked Open British National Bibliography, 2017, https://data.gov.uk/dataset/the-linked-open-british-national-bibliography.

Chapter 7

Open policy and collaboration with Wikimedia at the National Library of Wales

Jason Evans and Dr Dafydd Tudur

Since it first began to digitise items from its collections during the 1990s, the National Library of Wales has embraced digital technologies as a means of widening access to readers beyond the four walls of its iconic building in Aberystwyth. Facilitating access to its collections in this way has been a key strategic aim for the Library for many years, underpinned by the Theatre of Memory, a long-term vision of providing digital access to everything ever published in or about Wales.[1] In the last ten years, significant strides towards realising this vision have been made by delivering the large-scale digitisation projects Welsh Journals Online (https://journals.library.wales/) and Welsh Newspapers Online (http://newspapers.library.wales/), and allowing access to collections in a range of other formats – including photographs, artworks, maps, manuscripts and archives – through the Library's core digitisation programme and other projects.

The National Library of Wales from the outset committed to the principle of providing digital services that are free at the point of access. With the opportunities that digital technologies offer for reproduction, distribution and repurposing as well as viewing, the discussion inevitably led to questions of reuse. In 2009 the Library was among the first cultural organisations in the UK to share items from its collection on Flickr Commons (www.flickr.com/photos/llgc/), permitting their free and unrestricted use. In 2010, thousands of images were published on the Welsh Government's People's Collection Wales website (www.peoplescollection.wales/) under the Creative Archive Licence, similar to the CC BY-NC-SA licence.[2] In 2012, the Library made its most important policy decision in relation to the digitisation and reuse of its collections to date by declaring that it would not claim ownership of copyright in digital reproductions *per se*. This new position of 'what goes into the public domain would stay in the public domain', as described by Europeana, would have far-reaching consequences for the way in which the National Library of Wales's digitised collections were accessed and reused.

Since forming its current policy on copyright in digital reproductions, the National Library of Wales has faced what may possibly be the most challenging time in its history. On 26 April 2013, World Intellectual Property Day, the Library published a press release announcing its new position on copyright in digital reproductions. The Library did indeed make the news that day, but not because of its new policy. That afternoon, a fire broke out on the roof of its building in Aberystwyth causing millions of pounds' worth of damage. No one was injured, but the fire caused widespread disruption to the Library's services and activities as staff were relocated and assigned new tasks. During three years of recovery and reconstruction, budget cuts have led to restructuring and the number of staff working at the Library has reduced substantially. This combination hampered the implementation of the new policy and the realisation of its potential opportunities and benefits for the Library and the wider public.

The developments in policy at the Library paved the way for an alignment of strategy with Wikimedia UK. The Library had contributed to Wikimedia initiatives since 2012 and discussions between the two organisations resulted in the appointment of a joint-funded Wikipedian in Residence in 2015 with the broad aim of promoting free and open knowledge. The role of the Wikipedian in Residence and the use of Wikimedia platforms for sharing collections and engaging with users have enabled the Library to explore the opportunities arising from open access. Indeed, the National Library of Wales residency has since come to be regarded as one of the most successful to date. This case study explores the benefits, opportunities and challenges that have arisen from this collaboration between the National Library of Wales and Wikimedia UK, especially in relation to the provision of open access to digitised collections.

The collaboration

Wikimedia UK is a registered charity in the UK dedicated to collecting, developing, promoting and distributing open knowledge. The charity is the official UK chapter of the Wikimedia Foundation which oversees Wikipedia, Wikidata (the open data repository), Wikimedia Commons (the open media repository) and other community led projects. In 2010 a volunteer Wikipedian collaborated with the British Museum to pioneer an idea of placing

Wikipedians, or more broadly Wikimedians, into cultural institutions for a set period of time in order to encourage and develop open access policies and programmes along with encouraging contribution to Wikipedia articles. The Wikipedian in Residence scheme has since been rolled out in dozens of cultural institutions around the world, with many partners recording large increases in the use of their digital content through sharing openly with Wikipedia.

The National Library of Wales had contributed to Wikimedia initiatives before the residency began in January 2015. In 2013, 50 images relating to Monmouthshire were contributed to Wikipedia and the Library partnered Wikimedia UK and Europeana in developing a toolset to mass upload material from cultural organisations to Wikimedia Commons. Together with its new policy on copyright and digital reproductions, this led to the Library being awarded Wikimedia UK's GLAM (Galleries, Libraries, Archives and Museums) of the Year Award in 2013 for being 'a reliable supporter of the Wikimedia movement aims'.

Many aspects of the Wikimedia residency aligned with the Library's new open access policy and, more importantly, its 2014–17 strategic plan, *Knowledge for All*.[3] In previous residencies, Wikipedians were appointed from outside the organisations in which they would be based, but in this instance the Wikipedian was appointed from within the Library. The successful candidate, Jason Evans, had nine years' experience of working at the Library, primarily in the Reader Services department, providing guidance to users and carrying out research tasks. He brought to the post extensive knowledge of the Library's collections and services, an awareness of both user and staff needs and expectations, connections with staff throughout the organisation, as well as an understanding of the Library's management structures and processes. These have been key to Jason's success in the role of Wikipedian in Residence. Since January 2015, the residency has been extended twice, making the National Library of Wales's Wikipedian the longest residing Wikipedian in the UK since the scheme began in 2010.

The initial goals of the project included holding a number of events to train new Wikipedia editors. Another important goal was to work with library staff to share digital images on an open licence with Wikimedia Commons. Reuse of these images on Wikipedia and other Wikimedia projects would then be encouraged and monitored. The Wikipedian in Residence was also tasked with developing a sustainable mechanism through which the collaboration with Wikimedia could continue once the residency had ended.

Sharing digital images with Wikimedia

Sharing digital images from the Library's collections was to be central to the collaboration with Wikimedia UK, and the foundation for the activities associated with the residency. There were, however, important decisions to be made:

- Which digital collections would be shared with Wikimedia?
- How much content would be released?
- What quality (resolution) images would be released?

Selecting collections for release on an open licence

The clear goal for the Library was to increase the use and visibility of its digital images. Statistics from Wikimedia residencies at similar institutions demonstrated the potential of using Wikimedia platforms for sharing collections, recording total numbers of image views in the hundreds of thousands, if not millions, every month through the Wikipedia website.

Between March 2015 and January 2017, 11,240 images were uploaded to Wikimedia Commons as part of the residency.[4] The first batch of images uploaded to Wikimedia Commons were nearly 2000 photographs which the Library had already shared openly via Flickr Commons. From the beginning of the project, the Wikipedian and staff agreed that content released openly on one platform should be shared as widely as possible in order to maximise its impact and reach. Content which has been made available as public domain works or under open licences will be placed on third party platforms and websites sooner or later. In fact, some of those images which had been shared on Flickr Commons had already been transferred by users to Wikimedia Commons. These images and their metadata were checked and standardised. In taking a proactive approach to sharing open content, there was now an opportunity for the Library to ensure the quality of the images and accompanying metadata, and include links to its own records.

The majority of items shared on Wikimedia Commons have been instances where the Library owns copyright in the works (in their original format) or are regarded as public domain works. Apart from their copyright status, the key factor when selecting collections to release was its perceived potential for impact and reach through its inclusion in Wikipedia articles. The Library holds many more public domain works which are suitable for sharing in this way; the number uploaded to Wikimedia Commons was largely dictated by the availability of technical resources within the Library. In order to upload large image collections to Wikimedia Commons it was necessary to manipulate the image metadata into a format suitable for use with Wikimedia's mass upload tool.[5] Retrieving and preparing the collections for upload required the assistance of technical staff at the Library, and with tightening budgets and ever expanding workloads their time was at a premium.

A review into the Library's digitisation workflow provided an opportunity for the Wikipedian to work with Library staff to include the sharing of content to Wikimedia Commons and other third party websites as part of the digitisation workflow process, so that the suitability of any new digital content for sharing on Wikimedia Commons (and other strategically important third party platforms) is assessed and executed as part of the digitisation process. The sustainability of the Wikimedia residency was a key element of the project so the embedding of these practices into the core activities of the Library continues to be seen as a priority for both parties.

Quality of images uploaded

The issue that was most debated during the residency was the quality of images shared on Wikimedia Commons. The Library had adopted a 'two-tier' model for monetising its digitised collections, where lower resolution versions were available openly and higher quality versions released under terms of contract. To ensure consistency, images were therefore to be uploaded to Wikimedia Commons at the same quality, or resolution, as they appeared on the Library website.

When the residency began, the Library displayed images on its own website as thumbnail galleries. Images were expandable to between 800 and 1000 pixels at 72 dots per inch. Being aware that some respected cultural institutions were sharing images at a much higher resolution on Wikimedia Commons, the Wikipedian and the Library's digital access manager developed a business case for increasing substantially the resolution of the images shared by National Library of Wales, as part of a wider open access strategy. The business case focuses on the argument that releasing higher quality images, and providing open access in general, does not have a major negative impact on income generation, while clearly encouraging reuse. At the time of writing (spring 2017), the business case was being considered by the Library's senior staff.

Four-fifths (81%) of image uploads to Wikimedia Commons were 1000 pixels or less in size, with a smaller proportion of higher quality images uploaded in order to monitor impact (Figure 7.1 on the next page). Interestingly releasing larger quality images has had minimal impact on reuse of the images on Wikipedia, but reuse of the higher quality images outside Wikimedia projects is significantly higher.

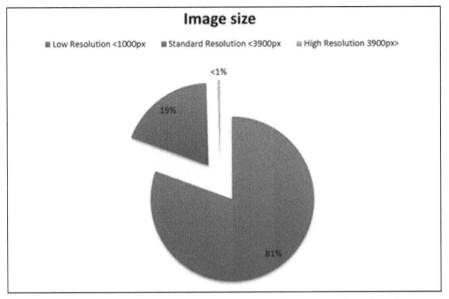

Figure 7.1 *The size of image uploads to Wikimedia Commons during the Wikimedia residency at the National Library of Wales (CC BY-SA)*
Source: WikiCommons

Impact

Reach

The number of times that images shared on Wikimedia Commons have been viewed in Wikipedia articles has been one of the clearest indicators of the residency's success. The main function of Wikimedia Commons is to provide a repository of openly licensed digital media which can be used on Wikipedia; the 'image views' statistic is the number of times an article or articles containing the image(s) in question are viewed. Wikipedia is consistently one of the most viewed websites in the world with hundreds of millions of unique visitors every month, and so there are few platforms that would be more suitable for placing collections in view of the widest possible audiences.

In March 2015 the first 576 images were uploaded to Wikimedia Commons. Analytics for the first month revealed 51,000 views of Wikipedia articles containing these images. This statistic continued to increase as more images were shared on Wikimedia Commons and embedded into Wikipedia. By the sixth month image views had reached 2.3 million per month and figures continued to rise month on month.

By August 2016 National Library of Wales images were being used in 4123 Wikipedia articles in 90 different languages, although 93% of page views came from the dominant English language Wikipedia. Over the 24-month period of the residency total image views hit 199 million (Figure 7.2).[6] To put this figure into contrast, the National Library of Wales main website received 1.3 million views during the same period.

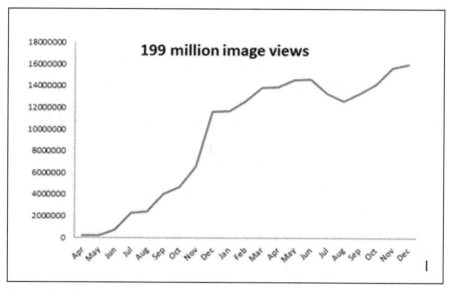

Figure 7.2   *The number of views of Wikipedia articles containing images from the first 576 uploaded to Wikimedia Commons at the National Library of Wales, April 2015 to December 2016*

It may be coincidence but the only drop in the number of monthly image views (June–August 2016) coincides with the only prolonged period that no new image were uploaded to Wikimedia Commons.

It would be misleading to suggest that this level of exposure can be gained simply by placing images on Wikimedia Commons. The Wikipedian credits the success of this project to a number of contributing factors:

- hand picking individual images and collections based on the image needs of Wikipedia and its community of editors
- using social media to advertise uploads to Wikimedia Commons and promote reuse
- working with local volunteers and the Wikipedia community to encourage the use of Library images in articles
- holding a number of 'edit-a-thon' events to create new Wikipedia content and incorporate the Library's digital content.[7]

The quality of the metadata associated with the images and their subsequent categorisation on Wikimedia Commons was also very important in paving the way for them to be included in Wikipedia articles. Another method employed by the Wikipedian was to hold a 'pic-a-thon' event where those who attended were trained specifically to insert images into imageless articles on Wikipedia.

Reuse

Wikimedia Commons is a repository of openly licensed digital media, which can be used not only on Wikipedia, but anywhere by anyone and in any way (subject to the terms specified in the licence information). Sharing collections on Wikimedia Commons therefore creates opportunities for them to be reused as well as viewed much more widely.

These are some examples of reuse of images shared during the residency:

- Culture 24 curated a digital gallery of Library content released to Wiki Commons.[8]
- Images reused in third party website as part of interactive historical timelines (Figure 7.3).[9]

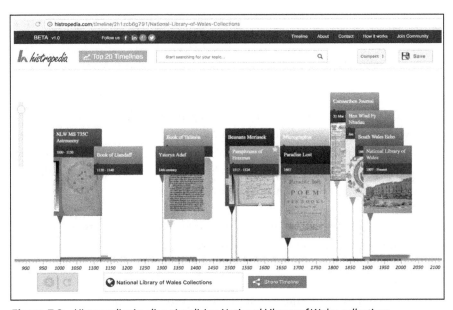

Figure 7.3   *Histropedia timeline visualising National Library of Wales collections*
Source: http://histropedia.com/timeline/2h1zcb6g791/National-Library-of-Wales-Collections © Histropedia Ltd., represented for the purposes of quotation

- Images included on a website dedicated to the study of Welsh Costume.[10]
- The book *50 Buildings that Built Wales* features public domain images from the National Library of Wales, found on Commons.[11]
- A map was used by an enthusiast as part of a georeferencing experiment.[12]
- A small local business used images in designs for commercial products such as T-shirts and mobile phone covers.[13]
- An image was included in a 2016 exhibition in Glasgow called Display at Your Own Risk.[14]
- Images were reused in an exhibition curated by the University of Wales in 2016 called Curious Travellers: Movement, Landscape, Art.[15]

A critic of open access could argue that those who reused this content may have paid for the right to use them if they were not freely available. Feedback from these users suggested that they were only able to reuse this content because it was free as their projects had very limited funding or none at all. For example, Dr Elizabeth Edwards, the curator of the exhibition Curious Travellers: Movement, Landscape, Art, commented: 'Open access is such a brilliant development – we're working to a shoestring budget for this, and would have really struggled (or only been able to show a couple of examples) if there was a charge involved'.

In all these instances of reuse, those involved were willing to credit the Library for the images, despite there being no obligation to do so. Many also contacted the Library as a matter of courtesy to inform us of their intentions and to confirm that they were free to reuse the content.

There is a growing body of evidence to suggest that the increase in reuse and the reputational benefits and opportunities for collaboration and engagement arising from sharing content openly would outweigh the level of income currently being generated from those collections.

It should be noted that it is currently not possible to monitor the reuse of digital content outside Wikimedia projects systematically. There is no data that can compare with the 'image views' that demonstrates how widely images are being reused, and for what purposes; this information is currently limited to case studies. Of the recorded instances of reuse above, 75% used the 20% of images with a resolution higher than 1000 pixels. While this clearly suggests that very low-resolution images will in many cases be unusable, it is believed that the development of standard and technical methods of measuring and monitoring reuse would strengthen the case in favour of increasing the quality of images shared on Wikimedia Commons and similar platforms.

Using, linking and enriching collections

Looking beyond the impact of image views and third party reuse of digital images, the Wikimedia collaboration has had many additional benefits. Edit-a-thon events have led to the creation of hundreds of new Wikipedia articles, but they have also served to provide volunteers with new skills, and helped engage members of the public with the Library's collections in order to create free accessible information. The Wikipedian also engaged with the Library's volunteer team, running a variety of projects including one creating 120 articles about 19th-century Welsh newspapers – a project that complemented the launch of the Library's revamped service Welsh Newspapers Online.

The National Library of Wales has also pioneered the idea of sharing cultural data openly via Wikidata. In April 2016 it became the first institution in the world to welcome a Wikidata visiting scholar.[16] By working closely with this Wikidata volunteer the Library was able to openly share and greatly enrich metadata for many of the digital items already shared with Wikimedia Commons, and other collections such as the Dictionary of Welsh Biography.[17] Working with volunteers the Library has also worked with the local county archives to combine two complementary datasets of local shipping records using Wikidata, which highlighted how linked open data can begin to create a rich web of interconnected historical collections. The marriage of volunteers and Wikidata allowed the Library to explore the advantages of creating linked data for its archive collections at no cost to the institution, while providing increasingly open access to its data. The Wikipedian in Residence has overseen the creation of around 15,000 Wikidata items for and about items in the Library's collections and, at the time of writing (Spring 2017), the Library had more Wikidata items for its open digital content than any other institution in the world.[18] Ultimately the aim is to create a sustainable environment where library staff, local volunteers and the wider wiki community have knowledge and skills to discover, enrich and reuse digital content from the Library's collections.

Exposure

The image view statistics from Wikipedia alone has generated a huge amount of exposure for the Library, but there has also been plenty of interest from the media, academia and the culture sector in the Library's Wikipedia edit-a-thons, open data initiatives and volunteer programmes.

The amount of media interest in the project was one unexpected aspect of the residency. The sharing of notable content has been covered by BBC Wales News and the Wikipedian has appeared on Welsh Radio on a number of occasions to discuss his work.[19] Online news outlets such as Vox and WalesOnline have run stories about the Library's sharing of open content.[20]

There has also been an increase in collaborations with other institutions as a result of the project. Several events were held in partnership with Welsh universities and county archives and the Wikipedian has worked closely with other heritage projects such as Wales for Peace (www.walesforpeace.org/), People's Collection Wales (https://www.peoplescollection.wales/) and the Urdd Eisteddfod (www.urdd.cymru/en/eisteddfod/). The success of the project has led to funding from the Welsh government to focus on improving aspects of the Welsh language Wikipedia and it is hoped that in time the success of the project will lead to more opportunities to collaborate and secure funding for further open access projects.

Conclusion

The collaboration with Wikimedia UK has had a key strategic influence on the Library since it began in January 2015. At a time when economic and political factors are putting pressure on cultural institutions to put up monetary barriers between the user and their use of its collections, the activities of the National Library of Wales's Wikimedia residency have been crucial in highlighting the wider benefits, both expected and unforeseen, of providing unrestricted access to works that are already in the public domain. The achievements of the residency in engagement and reach featured in the 2015–16 Annual Review[21] and initial consultation stages for the Library's Strategic Plan for 2017–20 underline the importance of the partnership with Wikimedia UK. These, combined with the initiatives currently under way, further consolidate the Library's role as the leading institution in Wales and more widely in the UK using Wikimedia platforms. It would appear that the achievements of the residency thus far may only be the first steps in realising the potential impact of this collaboration on the creation and accessibility of knowledge in and about Wales and its people.

Notes

1   National Library of Wales, The Theatre of Memory: Welsh print online, 2011,
    www.llgc.org.uk/fileadmin/fileadmin/docs_gwefan/amdanom_ni/
    dogfennaeth_gorfforaethol/dog_gorff_dog_thycS.pdf.

2   BBC, The Full Licence, 2014,
    www.bbc.co.uk/creativearchive/licence/full_licence.shtml.

3 National Library of Wales, *Knowledge for All: National Library of Wales Strategic Plan 2014–2017*, [2014], www.llgc.org.uk/fileadmin/fileadmin/docs_gwefan/amdanom_ni/dogfennaeth_gorfforaethol/corff_strat_KnowledgeforAll_2014_2017S.pdf.

4 Wikimedia Commons, Images from the Collection of the National Library of Wales, 2017, https://commons.wikimedia.org/wiki/Category:Images_from_the_collection_of_the_National_Library_of_Wales.

5 Wikimedia Commons, GLAMwiki Toolset, 2016, https://commons.wikimedia.org/wiki/Commons:GLAMwiki_Toolset.

6 Wikimedia Tool Labs, BaGLAMa 2: images uploaded as part of NLW–WMUK collaboration, 2017, https://tools.wmflabs.org/glamtools/baglama2/#gid=189&month=201612.

7 https://en.wikipedia.org/wiki/Wikipedia:How_to_run_an_edit-a-thon.

8 Culture 24, From the Head of a Fly to the Teeth of a Snail: ten of Robert Hooke's Micrographia Diagrams, 11 September 2015, www.culture24.org.uk/science-and-nature/art536635-from-the-head-of-a-fly-to-the-teeth-of-a-snail-robert-hookes-micrographia-diagrams.

9 National Library of Wales, Histropedia, n.d., http://histropedia.com/timeline/2h1zcb6g791/National-Library-of-Wales-Collections.

10 Welsh Costume, Llanover Album, 2016, https://welshhat.wordpress.com/influences-on-costume/royalty-nobility-and-gentry/lady-llanover/costume-images-1834/.

11 Stevenson, G. et al., *50 Buildings That Built Wales*, Graffeg, 2016.

12 Skrifennow: Georeferencing a tithe map and overlaying modern mapping in QGIS, 13 May 2015, http://skrifennow.blogspot.com/2015/05/georeferencing-tithe-map-and-overlaying.html.

13 Edwards, H., Hywel Edwards: Welsh visual artist, *Redbubble*, 2016, www.redbubble.com/people/billprice/shop/recent?ref=sort_order_change_recent.

14 Display At Your Own Risk: an experimental exhibition of digital cultural heritage, 26 April 2016, https://issuu.com/displayatyourownrisk/docs/display_at_your_own_risk_publicatio.

15 Oriel Sycharth Gallery, Future Exhibitions, 2016, www.glyndwr.ac.uk/OrielSycharthGallery/Whatson/FutureExhibitions/.

16 National Library of Wales, Our Wikidata Visiting Scholar, blog, 12 April 2016, www.llgc.org.uk/blog?p=11246.

17 Evans, J. and Cobb, S., How the World's First Wikidata Visiting Scholar Created

Linked Open Data for Five Thousand Works of Art, Wikimedia, 5 November 2016, https://blog.wikimedia.org/2016/11/05/wikidata-visiting-scholar-art-dataset/; National Library of Wales, Dictionary of Welsh Biography, 2009, http://yba.llgc.org.uk/en/index.html.

18   Zone47.com, Crotos – Callisto, n.d., http://zone47.com/crotos/callisto/.

19   BBC News, National Library Shares 2nd Century Ptolemy Map Image, 6 November 2015, www.bbc.co.uk/news/uk-wales-mid-wales-34746030.

20   Edwards, P., This 1853 Image Might Show the First Photobomb, Vox, 25 September 2015, www.vox.com/2015/9/25/9397733/first-photobomb; Williamson, D., Millions Have Seen These Historic Welsh Images a Librarian Has Helped Share on Wikipedia, WalesOnline, 9 February 2016, www.walesonline.co.uk/news/wales-news/millions-seen-historic-welsh-images-10859484.

21   National Library of Wales, *Annual Review 2015–16*, 2016, www.llgc.org.uk/fileadmin/fileadmin/docs_gwefan/amdanom_ni/ dogfennaeth_gorfforaethol/LLGC%20Annual%20Review%2015-16.pdf.

Chapter 8

Newcastle Libraries – the public library as a place to share culture

Aude Charillon

Introduction

Newcastle Libraries are the public libraries serving the citizens of the City of Newcastle upon Tyne, UK. Newcastle is the biggest city in the North East of England and its library service, in particular the City Library, attracts users from across the region and beyond. The City Library houses the local studies and family history collections – this section also regularly receives requests and enquiries from overseas customers.

In the early 2000s a funded project allowed Newcastle Libraries to digitise a large part of its local history photographic collections and to publish them on a dedicated website called Tyneside Life and Times. However, a few years later the website encountered technical difficulties and the photographs were moved to the Flickr image hosting platform in June 2009. When the Flickr albums were created the images' legal status appeared as the default copyright setting (Figure 8.1 on the next page).[1] Download was originally disabled but this was changed early on, although this particular feature was never publicised. Apart from the Torday collection (1000 photographs of 1960s–1970s Newcastle), which was digitised by a volunteer and uploaded to a new album, the historic images collection on Flickr has only been extended ad hoc.

Commons Are Forever

In 2015 I started developing the project Commons Are Forever at Newcastle Libraries, with support from the Carnegie UK Trust's Library Lab programme.[2] Commons Are Forever aimed to empower people by informing them of their rights to use and reuse works that are either in the public domain or available

Figure 8.1   *Newcastle Libraries at Flickr – 003382: Swing Bridge, Newcastle upon Tyne, 1889*
Source: No known copyright. Web page: www.flickr.com/photos/
newcastlelibraries/4075572881/in/album-72157622835504860/.
Copyright Yahoo Inc., represented for the purposes of quotation

under an open licence, and encourage them in turn to share their creations with others. The project took the form of a series of events where members of the public were invited to create their own artworks in workshops facilitated by local artists, while learning about copyright and where to find free-to-use content.

A secondary goal of the project was to firmly re-position the library service as a place for the sharing of culture. Public libraries are traditionally making knowledge and culture accessible through loaning materials to members of the community, but I believe raising awareness of works that are out-of-copyright – in the public domain and belonging to all – or under open licences is also part of libraries' role. It therefore made sense to me to use Commons Are Forever also to promote resources that are part of Newcastle Libraries' collections and have entered the public domain. Since we were promoting free-to-use materials as part of the project we also needed to apply those sharing principles to our collections and services.

The first step would be to re-label the local history images on Flickr from 'copyright – all rights reserved' to 'public domain'. In order to get agreement I started talking to colleagues in June 2015. It emerged that the issue was less about owning copyright over the digitised pictures and more about enforcing an indication of provenance: people who were not using our pictures for commercial ventures should be able to use them for free but be obliged to mention they were from our collections. However, it was felt that claiming copyright was still important because we were the keepers of the collection: if people want to make money from using our pictures then the library should get something too, and it should be clear that the images came from Newcastle Libraries. As we were selling copies of our pictures, the potential loss of income was mentioned – at a time of budget reductions even the small amount we were making could become significant.

After this initial meeting the conversation stalled as changing this particular policy, which had been in place for a while, was not part of the team's priorities. The topic was picked up on several occasions over the following year and the number of people involved in the discussions was extended to the wider group of librarians. To get colleagues to understand why I wanted the Flickr images' status changed from in-copyright to public domain I used arguments such as: 'because you're trying to claim rights that you probably don't have, what we are doing now is slightly illegal but also ethically wrong'!

Sharing data and information

Towards the end of the Commons Are Forever project the focus moved from sharing creative works to sharing data and information collected by the library service. We released performance statistics and usage figures as open data – using the UK Open Government Licence, which allows anyone to reuse the information in any way, as long as the source of the information is credited. In April 2016 we ran a one-day hack-a-thon when we invited members of the community to 'play' with our open data. For the occasion we were also given permission to publish 31 digitised historical maps of Newcastle from the libraries' collections – in the public domain, clearly labelled as such in a Flickr album. The maps proved quite popular, with several participants using them to superimpose 'old Newcastle' to a current map to highlight the evolution of the city centre.

What happened with the maps helped to show colleagues what releasing our information and content meant, and more importantly that it did not harm the library service. On the contrary, it was interesting to see what citizens had done with our maps when appropriating them – reusing them in ways we had not thought of and contributing to the visibility and reach of our collections.

In August 2016 we changed the status of our local history images on Flickr to 'public domain'. Each album now states:

These images are, to the best of our knowledge, in the public domain. You are welcome to use them in any way you like – we would love it if you could say you got them from the Newcastle City Library Photographic Collection. If you want to use the images for commercial purposes we can provide you with a high quality digital image for a fee – just contact us.

On the spur of the moment, it was also decided to move the Torday collection (the copyright of which had been assigned to Newcastle Libraries) into the public domain – under the Creative Commons Zero (CC0) licence.

We were pleased to see this initiative bear fruit a few months later, with an article in a local newspaper about Newcastle's old Odeon cinema featuring several of our Flickr images – all in the public domain but nevertheless including the statement 'from the Newcastle City Library Photographic Collection'.[3]

Around the same time we changed the status of our local history images on Flickr to 'public domain', we also decided to stop using Open Government Licence for our open data and use CC0 instead, making it even easier for our information to be reused.

Open by default

In December 2016 we went further: we librarians agreed that in the future all Newcastle Libraries collections and documents published online would be made open by default. All public domain materials digitised from our collections will be clearly labelled as such when published. Materials created by library staff – images, event pictures, information booklets, training guides and so on – will be published under a Creative Commons Attribution licence. In 2017 we will start making more of our content available via platforms such as Flickr and GitHub.

Notes

1   Flickr, Newcastle Libraries: albums, 2017,
     www.flickr.com/photos/39821974@N06/albums/.

2   Newcastle City Council, Commons Are Forever, 14 December 2016,
     www.newcastle.gov.uk/leisure-libraries-and-tourism/events/commons-are-forever.

3   Oldfield, L., Newcastle's Odeon Cinema: rare photos and original plans of city
     centre landmark, *Chronicle Live*, 1 November 2016,
     www.chroniclelive.co.uk/news/history/newcastles-odeon-cinema-rare-photos-
     12109787.

Chapter 9

Developing open licensing at the National Library of Scotland

Gill Hamilton and Fred Saunderson

Introduction

From unplanned, somewhat opportunistic beginnings, the National Library of Scotland has been openly licensing resources since 2008. The Library's approach to open licensing has taken a more strategic and considered direction since 2014 by developing structured policies and procedures. In this case study we examine this, from the Library's early openness steps driven primarily by external factors to the Library's more recent approaches to being open, which derive from greater internal drivers while continuing to be informed and inspired by external developments. We argue that this development process demonstrates how, even when setting out initially with no openness plan, cultural heritage organisations can develop open approaches and use open licences successfully.

Exploring external drivers

The National Library of Scotland's earliest use of open licences begins with the web. The Library's first website was developed in the mid-1990s, driven by the potential to reach a larger, more diverse audience.[1] Mainly text-based, this first website iteration had only a few images, including the Library's logo and a few of the Library's treasured collection items.

This lack of imagery was not unusual for the time. Expensive, low-resolution (compared with today) digital cameras were in their infancy and just being introduced to the non-professional market. Tools to manipulate digital images were basic. Domestic connection speeds were slow, between 28 and 56 kilobytes per second, more than 1000 times slower than the fibre speeds (up to 76 megabytes per second) we are familiar with today, so users were likely to be dissuaded by image and data-rich websites.

All text and images on this first website iteration were marked '© Copyright Trustees of the National Library of Scotland'. Open licensing, largely limited at this time to the software industry, was not considered. Easily accessible, public-focused, generic open licences, such as Creative Commons licences, were not yet available. This type of 'all rights reserved' copyright notice was used less by design and more by default: there were no real alternatives, nor was the intellectual openness of this nascent communication channel high on the organisational agenda.

Digitisation efforts at the Library commenced around this time, progressing in an ad hoc manner with basic scanners and digital camera equipment. The initial aim of this work was to create images for the website and for exhibitions. However, realising that outputs of digitisation could improve the Library's reach beyond its physical home in Edinburgh, greater investment was made into funding expertise and equipment to advance digitisation. Several projects were established to digitise unique or rare 'treasure' items, including:

- the Chepman and Myllar Prints, a collection of the only known copies of nine of the earliest books printed in Scotland[2]
- the last letter of Mary Queen of Scots, written four hours before her beheading in 1587
- the earliest surviving detailed maps of Scotland made by Timothy Pont in the late 16th century.[3]

Although the open movement was gaining traction and the Creative Commons framework was growing in popularity at this time, the Library continued to publish digital material under an 'all rights reserved' banner. It was not until 2008 that two activities initiated discussions about how the Library's digitised content could be licensed for the first time.

Flickr

In January 2008 the image sharing website Flickr launched, in collaboration with the Library of Congress, the Flickr Commons initiative. This was a platform for enabling cultural heritage organisations to make their digitised collections more widely and freely available. The Library of Congress made more than 3000 images available at launch (there are now more than 28,000 images) and immediately benefited in its reach and engagement with the public as the images were used and reused.[4] The only condition to participation in Flickr Commons was that contributing organisations had to supply content free from copyright restrictions using the statement 'no known copyright restriction'.

For the National Library to participate in Flickr Commons and realise similar benefits of sharing collections required careful consideration of the implication of Flickr's licensing policy and the *raison d'être* and ethos of the Commons. It also required a rethink in the way in which digital images were licensed by the Library and challenged us to consider whether it was right, or indeed helpful to our strategic aims, to limit access and reuse of material paid for by public funds.

There was much discussion in the Library about the risks and benefits of Flickr Commons, with one of the biggest concerns being the loss of potential future income from images that were made openly available. Ultimately we decided to engage with Flickr Commons, but with a considerable concession to the perceived risk of lost income generation. The Library published more than 2000 images under the 'no known copyright restrictions' terms of reuse, but restricted the images to just 300 pixels wide (Figure 9.1). This compromise aimed

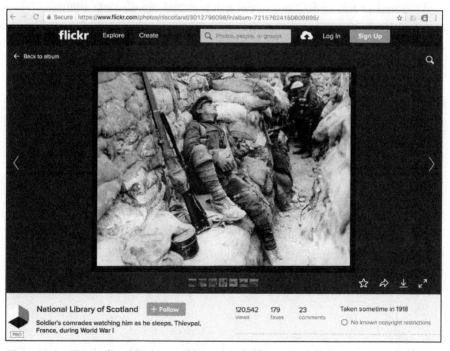

Figure 9.1   *Photo of a soldier's comrades watching him as he sleeps in Thiepval, France, during World War 1, National Library of Scotland at Flickr*
Source: No known copyright restriction. Web page:
https://www.flickr.com/photos/nlscotland/3012796098

to exploit the advantages of openness while attempting to retain control over income generation opportunities derived from the commercial licensing of higher quality images. Despite this mixed approach, the Library's tentative steps into open licensing proved a major success, with the images published to the Commons having received to date over 15 million views and thousands of comments and likes, indicating deeper levels of engagement.

When the Library loaded these 2000 images onto Flickr Commons we did not retrospectively convert the licence on the same resources on our website to 'no known copyright restriction', however. Through this omission, the Library unintentionally introduced further ambiguity and complexity.

The Internet Archive

In 2008, in a drive to increase output and the speed at which content was made available to the public, the Library contracted the digitisation services of the not-for-profit Internet Archive. At this time the Library lacked the infrastructure to undertake mass digitisation on our own and did not have facilities and processes in place to publish material rapidly once digitised. The Internet Archive, on the other hand, had a high digitisation throughput and was able to publish the outputs of digitisation on its website within 48 hours, but a condition of using the Internet Archive's digitisation services was that all digitised content published on its website must be open. As with the 'no known copyright restrictions' Flickr Commons statement, the Internet Archive's requirement to use an open licence had to be reviewed and considered by the Library. Again, concerned about protecting perceived future income, the Library was satisfied that its financial and commercial interests would be protected by the CC BY-NC-SA licence. When the Library later published the resources digitised by Internet Archive on its own website, it was the first time that the Library used open licences on its own domain. The Internet Archive's requirement led to the CC BY-NC-SA licence becoming the Library's default licence for digitised resources, but there was still no formal, agreed licensing policy and procedure in place.

Europeana

While the Library's early use of open licences and rights statements with digitised resources was driven largely by Flickr Commons and the Internet Archive, use of open licences for metadata was driven by the development of the Europeana initiative. At its core, Europeana (http://pro.europeana.eu/) is a metadata aggregator and provider of a unified portal (www.europeana.eu/portal/en) for accessing the digital collections of European cultural heritage organisations. Europeana's developers needed to be able to reuse the metadata of participating organisations in order to build this portal, develop services, and transform metadata into linked open data. However, negotiating with hundreds of different Europeana partners to agree suitable reuse licenses would have been time consuming, resource intensive and unsustainable.

As a Europeana partner, the Library participated in workshops and discussions in 2012 that led to the development of the Europeana Data Exchange Agreement, which sought to address this problem.[5] The agreement requires that organisations participating in Europeana must supply metadata under a Creative Commons Zero (CC0) licence or waiver. The Library signed the agreement and has subsequently supplied metadata to the project under the CC0 licence or waiver.

Advancing internal drivers

Driven by the requirements and best practice of Flickr Commons, the Internet Archive and Europeana, the Library's approach to licensing digitised content and digital collections metadata was by 2013 fairly ad hoc. Licensing and reuse approaches remained undocumented on the whole, and there was little to unify the organisation's approach to reuse or to provide clarity to staff or users about our overarching policy towards digital licensing.

In 2013 and 2014 the development of three new roles – a digital access manager, a Wikimedian in Residence, and an intellectual property specialist – enabled us to formalise our reuse and licensing approaches for the first time throughout the organisation. We were able to do this largely because for the first time there were dedicated staff within the Library tasked with developing key areas such as access to digital content and copyright and reuse conditions.

Wikimedian in Residence as advocate for open

Part-funded by Wikimedian UK, Dr Ally Crockford had a unique position in her role as Wikimedian in Residence to act as advocate for the use of open licences. Unlike the aforementioned ventures, where specified reuse or licensing terms were requirements of digitisation or dissemination partners, Ally acted as a catalyst and facilitator for improving access to the Library's collections. Rather than task the Library with committing to a particular licence for a particular project, the Wikimedian was in a position to promote the benefits of clear, consistent and open reuse terms in a much broader sense.

The Wikimedian's advocacy and catalyst position was supported by the functions of the new digital access manager and intellectual property specialist roles. Unlike the Wikimedian, these roles were less focused on promotion and more on formalisation and supporting the Library's stable, long-term development. In order to place digital material such as digitised images on Wikimedia Commons, the image and content database that serves Wikipedia, among others, a suitably open licence must be used. Wikimedia Commons will not permit material licensed in any manner more restrictive than a Creative Commons Attribution ShareAlike (CC BY-SA) licence. In summer 2014 the Wikimedian obtained permission from the Library's senior leadership to undertake a test release of existing digitised imagery onto Wikimedia using the most open statement possible, the CC0 licence or waiver. Crucially, senior management permitted a high quality, 2500-pixel-wide version of these test images to be released. Ally released over 1000 images and associated metadata to Wikimedia, taking a slice of content from material previously published under the more restrictive CC BY-NC-SA licence on the Library's own website (Figure 9.2).[6]

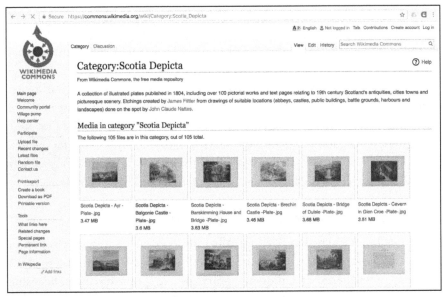

Figure 9.2   *Selection of National Library of Scotland's WikiCommons images*
Source: https://commons.wikimedia.org/wiki/Category:Scotia_Depicta

Owing to the way that Wikimedia Commons displays copyright information for faithful reproductions of public domain works and because the Library used the

CC0 licence, these test images unintentionally ended up being displayed on Wikimedia Commons as public domain. In part because of this small but significant outcome, this test release was a major shift for the Library. Up to this point, focus had remained on retaining rights in images and protecting the organisation's ability to generate income through reuse licensing. Nevertheless, the release was successful in two important ways. First, it promoted access to the material, with over 340 of the images included in more than 850 Wikipedia articles by February 2017. The articles in which the Library's resources are featured have been viewed more than 65 million times.[7] Although each image is not necessarily viewed on each page visit, it nevertheless accounts for an incredible growth in potential and likely access to the material. Indeed, as the digitised images already existed, this increased level of access came at no new cost to the Library.

Second, the test gave library staff the additional information they needed to understand what being more open with digital content might look like. This experience, combined with past experiences with Flickr Commons, the Internet Archive, Europeana, the advocacy role of the Wikimedian, and the formalising roles of the digital access manager and intellectual property specialist, led the Library finally to develop a formal, coherent and informed licensing and reuse policy.

Developing the open licensing policy

In 2014 library staff developed an open licensing policy after the test release to Wikimedia, building on an outline prepared in 2013 by the digital access manager. It proposed that:

- by moving from CC BY-NC-SA by default to CC BY by default there would be greater use and reuse of Library collections so the Library would deliver on its strategic commitment to provide universal access to knowledge
- the Library's role in supporting the digital economy of Scotland should enable commercial reuse of material
- the Library could still generate income even when content was openly licensed
- it was unethical to continue to claim restrictive rights in digitised versions of public domain works
- participation in Europeana and other linked open data initiatives was impossible, or would be severely curtailed, while there was no policy for

metadata licensing, and that to date these ventures (such as participation in Europeana) had proceeded by exception rather than by default, an unsustainable method for the longer term.

In 2014, as a result of the arguments put forward and experiences learned from the work of the Wikimedian, the intellectual property specialist and digital access manager specified and produced the Library's Metadata and Digital Content Licensing Policy.[8] Unlike previous ventures, this was an attempt to establish a uniform and organisation-wide approach to reuse licensing, rather than one driven by a specific project or set of content. Under the policy, the Library defined two 'default' licences:

- Creative Commons Attribution (CC BY) to be applied to 'access quality' digital content and 'core' metadata
- Creative Commons Attribution NonCommercial ShareAlike (CC BY-NC-SA) to be applied to 'master quality' digital content and 'extended' metadata.

As well as the default licences, a number of possible exceptions were specified, for example to apply distinct licensing terms where required by third party rights owners, contracts or agreements.

A number of options for the licence framework were debated within the Library during this time. Lessons learned from the trial release to Wikimedia, in particular the inadvertent labelling of images as public domain, led the Library to avoid using the CC0 statement for images, as this was determined to be excessive in our area of risk: maintaining a trial of provenance.

Senior management agreed the policy in 2014 and it was a major advance for the Library. In particular, for the first time this policy gave us a framework on which any digital material could be given a reuse licence. However, the policy noticeably inherited a high degree of complexity, thanks to the Library's assiduous balancing of benefit and risk and the desire to meld the policy where possible to our status quo: the use of the CC BY-NC-SA licence. The policy divides material into parcels, largely as a method to mitigate risks. Terms such as 'core metadata' and 'access quality digital content' were incorporated into the final structure, which added to the policy's complexity.

Outcomes of the policy

With the Metadata and Digital Content Licensing Policy agreed and in place work has continued on open licensing and promoting access and reuse of the Library's digital collections:

- CC BY is now the Library's default licence for all digitised two-dimensional resources and metadata (except where there are legal, contractual or other limitations, or where the content is 'master quality' content).
- Work has been completed to convert existing licences retrospectively from CC BY-NC-SA to CC BY on more than 4 million images in the Library's Digital Gallery (http://digital.nls.uk/), where there are no relevant restrictions. This has been reasonably straightforward and quick to achieve for the majority of images, in particular those relating to digitised published texts of public domain works, but pockets of content that prove challenging to convert remain. Some of these issues relate to uncertainty about who the copyright holder is, often because of lack of documentation with early digitisation projects or obligations set out in existing agreements with third parties.
- With the increasing interest in data analytics through text and data mining, the policy was clarified to ensure machine-generated texts output as a result of optical character recognition are licensed with a CC BY licence (Figure 9.3 on the next page). Some of the Library's digitised texts have since been used in natural language processing and semantic tagging projects.[9]
- In December 2016, the Library launched data.nls.uk, a service to provide free access to its data under either CC0 or CC BY licences. Initially, 14 datasets were made available, with plans to release dozens more in 2017.
- During 2017, as part of its review of its digital production processes, the Library will fully automate how it distributes its openly licensed digitised resources and metadata to Wikimedia Commons and Europeana.

Conclusion

Although complex, the policy that emerged in 2014 represents a significant and useful step forward for the Library. From our first digitisation and online access efforts in the 1990s through to 2014, digitised content was made available without an agreed or clear policy for reuse. The Library's use of licences, while increasingly open during this period, was driven not by an internal policy linked to strategy, but instead by marrying organisational ambitions with the requirements and practices of external drivers. With the catalyst role of the Wikimedian in Residence and the formalising roles of the digital access

Set display mode to: Zoom image

Figure 9.3   *Theatre poster with CC BY licence*
Source: http://digital.nls.uk/74535032

manager and intellectual property specialist, the Library from 2013 obtained the scope, capacity and desire to formalise our use of licensing and rights statements.

The current reuse policy is not perfect, and the Library's approach to reuse will continue to evolve. However, strong external drivers followed by informed internal drivers allowed the Library to move from a fully closed digital reuse environment, to an ad hoc semi-open approach, and finally to a formalised and more open environment over the past years.

Notes

1   Web Archive, National Library of Scotland, 1996,
    web.archive.org/web/19970212054659/http://www.nls.uk/index.htm.

2   National Library of Scotland, First Scottish Books, 2006,
    http://digital.nls.uk/firstscottishbooks/.

3   National Library of Scotland, Pont Maps of Scotland, ca. 1583–1614, n.d.,
    http://maps.nls.uk/pont/.

4   Springer, M., Dulabahn, B., Michel, P., Natanson, B., Reser, D., Woodward, D.
    and Zinkham, H., *For the Common Good: the Library of Congress Flickr Pilot
    Project*, Library of Congress, 2008, www.loc.gov/rr/print/flickr_report_final.pdf.

5   Europeana Professional, Data Exchange Agreement, 26 September 2016,
    http://pro.europeana.eu/files/Europeana_Professional/DEA/Data%
    20Exchange%20Agreement.pdf.

6   Wikimedia Tool Labs, BaGLAMa 2: images uploaded as part of NLW–WMUK
    collaboration, 2017,
    https://tools.wmflabs.org/glamtools/baglama2/#gid=189&month=201612.

7   Wikimedia Tool Labs, Images from National Library of Scotland, 2017,
    tools.wmflabs.org/glamtools/baglama2/index.html#gid=157&month=201702.

8   National Library of Scotland, Metadata and Digital Content Licensing Policy,
    2016, www.nls.uk/media/1233752/2016-metadata-digital-licencing-policy.pdf.

9   Osborne, N., January 2016 Meetup at the National Library of Scotland, OK
    Scotland, 1 February 2016, https://scot.okfn.org/2016/02/01/
    january-2016-meetup-at-the-national-library-of-scotland/.

Chapter 10

The Wellcome Library

Christy Henshaw, Digitisation Programme Manager,
Wellcome Library

Introduction

The Wellcome Library is one of the world's major resources for the study of medical history. We are primarily a special collections library, with a wide range of materials dating from ancient times to the present day. We embarked on a long-term mass digitisation programme in 2010, and over the past six years we have digitised – and worked with our partners to digitise – over 25 million images as well as hundreds of hours of digital video. We also collect born-digital archival and published works and clinical and biomedical digital imagery.

'Good health makes life better. We want to improve health for everyone by helping great ideas to thrive.' Guided by this core philosophy of the Wellcome Trust, of which we are a part, the Library's aim becomes clear: to create an environment for these great ideas to thrive. To do this we showcase a diversity of experiences of health across time and in different cultures and settings and make it possible for people to understand those experiences better. We can only achieve this by maximising the reach and impact of our collections.

'Going digital' is not enough – we must also ensure that all our digital assets are as open and accessible as possible, embracing the diversity in our audiences, and ensuring that we don't construct barriers where there need be none. This thread runs through everything we do – from collecting our materials, to describing, arranging and classifying them, to our user interface design and system development – and connects us to our users, their ideas and their creations. Open licensing is a key strategy to keeping this thread intact.

Unlocking 20th-century content

The limited availability of 20th-century material online – the so-called 20th-century 'black hole'[1] – is a particular pain point for any cultural heritage institution wishing to open up its collections to a public audience (or any audience). This was the case before the EU Directive on Orphan Works and the UK implementation of the Orphan Works Licensing scheme, and it remains the case today.[2] The risk to collection holders of orphan works are only a part of the problem. The problem is also the vast number of individual rights holders who probably could be traced, but who are ambiguous or difficult to verify, have no current details available online or in any database, and who – even where they have been traced – are unlikely to respond to a request for permission to digitise and publish online. For many collections, copyright clearance according to the official guidelines is highly inefficient and leads to huge expenses of time and effort, for little return. For most collections, the sheer number of rights holders – traceable or not – makes it simply too expensive to attempt to contact rights holders for large-scale digitisation purposes.

We have carried out multiple copyright clearance procedures for a range of rights holders such as literary authors, scientists, artists, publishers, politicians, actors, public organisations, commercial organisations and photographers. We have analysed the risks related to unpublished letters, manuscript drafts, monographs, ephemera, sketches, posters, government literature, directories, offprints, news clippings, illustrations, serials and many more in our copyright clearance journey.

We have worked on our own, developing processes and procedures that we felt constituted 'due diligence', and we have worked in collaboration with rights organisations such as the Authors' Licensing and Collecting Society (ALCS) and the Publishers Licensing Society (PLS). We have combined forces with our peers – university and research libraries with similar aims to our own – and participated in research studies. We have enlisted the help of copyright experts, and participated in government consultations on copyright legislation. Over this time we have evolved our approach to copyright clearance and our licensing strategy for the digital assets we produce whether they are in- or out-of-copyright.

Our takedown policy

We treat different collections differently, and the sections below provide some details around this. However, all of our in-copyright digitised works are subject to our takedown policy.[3] If any copyright holder requests that we remove an item, we will do so immediately, and then proceed to investigate the request.

To date, we have had a couple of takedown requests related to copyright, and these items are now unavailable online. In such cases we will also ensure that copies are removed from any of our project partners who may also be making content available.

Commercial publications

We have concluded that there is no good solution for clearing copyright for mass digitisation for materials that reside largely in the domain of commercial publishers. We have some hopes for extended collective licensing, although at the time of writing (Spring 2017) rights organisations are many months – probably years – away from implementing this scheme.[4] In the meantime, we reluctantly avoid digitising monographs or pamphlets that were published from the mid-20th century onwards, and carry out only very limited digitisation of early 20th-century materials in this category.

In 2012, we participated in a pilot project with the ALCS and PLS to test whether we could create a scalable methodology for clearing copyright of published works in a mass digitisation project. The objective of the pilot was to copyright clear and digitise over 2000 books dating from 1850 to 1990 on the history of genetic research.

The ALCS and PLS identified in-commerce and in-copyright works using the ARROW system (www.arrow-net.eu/) combined with their own databases. They then identified and traced rights holders for the books that were out of print but still in-copyright (or likely to be in-copyright). If rights holders could not be traced after a due diligent search, the book was classed as an orphan work. Full details of the project in the form of a final report are available online.[5]

From this collection of books selected solely by subject, most rights holders were ostensibly traceable, with only 10% of titles resulting in an orphan works status (Table 10.1 on the next page). However, even with this relatively high rate of traceability and the response rate we received (whether positive or negative), we realised that the level of effort required was simply too expensive to sustain beyond the pilot.

The cost of the project to the Wellcome was around £45,000. This was likely artificially low as we had a fixed price agreement with the ALCS, but the amount of time required to identify and trace copyright holders was greater than anticipated. The number of titles for which we received a definitive response from rights holders was 691, so the cost per *successfully traced* title was £65.12 – or for each *approved for digitisation* title, the cost was £92.78 per work (bearing in mind

Table 10.1   *Breakdown of the rights holders of 2025 titles at the Wellcome Institute published between 1850 and 1990*

Rights holder	Total
Out-of-copyright	15%
In commerce	13%
Permission granted by at least one rights holder	24%
Permission denied by at least one rights holder	10%
Orphan works	10%
No response (after three tries)	18%
Other	10%

n = 2025

that some approvals were subject to restrictions such as no download as PDF, or private use only). When we consider that we have tens of thousands of books in this date range in our collections, at this rate the copyright clearance work alone would cost us millions of pounds in addition to the cost of retrieving, assessing, preparing, tracking, digitising and electronically preserving the items.

We digitised and published online all titles identified for the pilot except those that were in commerce or where permission was denied by at least one rights holder. Sometimes the author granted permission and the publisher refused permission. As we could not be sure who owned the rights for digital reproduction, we always removed such titles from the scope.

Publicly funded grey literature

For publicly funded works we have attempted to gain permission from rights holders in the past and received a 100% approval rate to publish online. This has led us to adapt our approach so that we no longer request permission *per se* for such material, although we endeavour to contact rights holding bodies to alert them to our plans. We can therefore initiate contact without imposing huge lead times waiting for responses.

A few years ago we digitised our Medical Officer of Health reports for London, and most local authorities assigned an Open Government Licence for the 20th-century reports (a couple opted for a Creative Commons NonCommercial licence).[6] However, even though we only needed to communicate with the 32 London boroughs and the City of London for that project, it took us a year to secure final permission for some of these areas mainly because of the length of time it can take local authorities to work through their internal processes, and the low priority such a request appears to have in these busy departments.

We are currently digitising the remaining Medical Officer of Health reports for the whole UK – around 65,000 reports in addition to the 5500 London reports already online. We estimate 130 county archives or equivalent manage the rights to these reports. Under the revised strategy we contacted rights holders to alert them to the project, rather than requesting formal permission. This 'light touch' approach has enabled organisations to respond informally and therefore quickly (sometimes within minutes of our e-mail arriving). In this way, we have succeeded in raising awareness on a local level and have had several offers to fill gaps in our sequence from collections held by the local archives. Where we have received no response we will continue to digitise and make available online without interruption. If we receive a response refusing permission or placing restrictions on use (we have had no such response to date), we will omit the relevant reports from the project.

Public health posters

In 2008–9 we attempted to copyright clear our collection of nearly 3000 international AIDS campaign posters, which were produced between the 1970s and 1990s. We were able to identify a possible 1800 rights holders, and found some sort of contact details for 656 of them. It took over a year and some 130 days of staff time to complete the clearance work. Although we were able to trace at least one rights holder for 80% of the posters, we only received replies covering 12% of posters (Table 10.2). The 'publishers' – usually AIDS-specific or general health charities – were more likely to be traced; it was much more difficult to trace creators of embedded rights such as imagery and artwork, either because they were uncredited and could not be identified, or because the creator did not have any online presence. Publishers and creators who were not based in Europe, North America or Australasia were particularly difficult to track down.

Table 10.2 *Breakdown of types of copyright clearance given for 2986 international AIDS campaign posters at the Wellcome Institute*

Type of permission	Total
Permission granted by at least one rights holder	10%
Permission denied by at least one rights holder	2%
Orphan works	16%
No response	69%
Other	3%

n = 2986

We published online all images except those where permission was refused by at least one rights holder.

Unpublished archives

The vast majority of our archival collections are unpublished literary works created or collected by medical persons, organisations and societies. Our main concern with publishing this type of material online is, naturally, data protection and privacy.[7] Copyright is also an issue, as these collections fall largely within the period of the author's life + 70 years. The 2039 rule, which was unfortunately not rescinded in 2014, is illogical, providing no cut-off whatsoever for unpublished literary works, so 'life + 70 years' is our guideline for considering copyright clearance for this material.[8] However, we feel it is imperative that this material, which is completely unique and physically accessible only at the Wellcome Library, is made available freely to the public. We have established a specific approach for these collections to deal with the sheer scale of rights holders represented in the typical archival collection.

We undertake rights clearance for archival collections on two fronts:

- *Creators of the archive collection* are the creators of the collection or their heirs who are likely to own the rights to a significant proportion of a collection, for example, the Galton Institute for the Eugenics Society Archive, or James Watson for the James Watson Papers. We attempt to locate and request permission from these individuals and organisations wherever possible. So far, we have been able to gain permission in all cases where the rights owner could be tracked down.
- *Third party rights owners* are the various rights owners whose works are included in the archive by virtue of their relationship with the collection's creator(s), or by the creator's collecting activities. This can include anything from a single piece of correspondence to a newspaper clipping to examples of patient art; there is simply too much variety to describe fully here.

For third party rights we developed a process of risk assessment that narrows down our efforts to what we consider to be high-risk rights holders. In a nutshell, these are rights holders who are highly public figures, known actively to defend their copyright, and/or have a literary estate or equivalent which is income generating. This process relies on the knowledge and judgement of the archivists and other staff involved in making these assessments. When we worked with partners to digitise collections outside the Wellcome Library, our partners provided that expertise in assessing the risks for their own collections. In this way, we can narrow down thousands of potential rights holders to tens of high-risk copyright holders (or even fewer for older archives, or archives with few third party rights).

When we first started writing to third party rights holders we were pleasantly surprised at the positive responses we got back – not just giving us approval to digitise the content, but actively supporting the project and its aims to make the information freely available online. One difficulty for rights holders was knowing what exactly was in the archive. We would provide a description, but we also found ourselves digitising content in order to send them printouts or digital copies so they could see what was there before granting permission.

The rate of success in tracking down rights holders and receiving responses is fairly high as we are selecting rights holders who are by their nature well known. We still encounter the odd orphan work. A paper on our first major digitisation project to employ this method provides all the details including rates of response.[9] The headline is that we had 2 refusals out of 103 replies for that project, and since then we have had no refusals. Over the course of the last few years we have received three takedown requests related to archival materials, although none of these requests cited copyright as the reason for the takedown. We feel this approach allows us to work in a way that is financially sustainable while making this unique content available, and ensures that rights holders who are most likely to be affected by our actions are given the opportunity to refuse permission.

Licensing

Our licensing regime for digitised content has changed over the years as we have learned more about the risks involved, and about the types of use we want to support. Our vision has become more explicit around a mission to disseminate information about the history of medicine as freely and easily as possible to encourage creative uses, including commercial exploitation where appropriate. We now assign a Creative Commons Attribution licence for content we own the rights to or a public domain mark for those that are out-of-copyright. We are in the process of converting legacy content to one or the other of these licences, so there may still be some inconsistency to current users.

To date, we have made orphan works and other in-copyright works for which we have been unable to gain explicit permission available under a Creative Commons Attribution NonCommercial licence. The rationale for this was that we felt there would be less risk to potential rights holders if we restrict commercial exploitation of these surrogates. An alternative method is simply to declare the work as 'not copyright cleared', provide the user with the data we have on the work, and put the onus on the user to identify and contact rights holders where they see fit. We will be testing this approach on a small set of posters and postcards in 2017.

When we ask rights holders for permission to digitise and publish online, we ask for the most open licence we feel makes sense for a particular collection. We believe a Creative Commons Attribution licence covers the vast majority of cases. However, where it is clear that content might have a commercial value to the rights holder, we would likely ask for a Creative Commons Attribution NonCommercial licence so the material can be used freely for personal and academic purposes, but does not prevent the rights holder from exercising an exclusive right to exploit the content commercially.

Conclusion

Our approach to rights clearance and licensing will continue to develop as the nature of our work evolves and the legal landscape changes. However, we know from experience that rights holders of works created for personal, educational and other not-for-profit purposes are highly unlikely to refuse permission, and in fact commonly welcome the possibility of the material being made openly available. We know that revenant rights holders are unlikely to come forward and make themselves known. On the rare occasions this happens, and a request is made to remove the content, our takedown policy works to the rights holders' satisfaction.

The case is different with commercially published works. Here the risks are higher, raising the bar for due diligence to a point that is unsustainable. Extended collective licensing might provide a solution to this in due course, and we welcome further development of this option by copyright and licensing bodies.

Notes

1   Gómez, P. U. and Keller, P., The Missing Decades: the 20th century black hole in Europeana, blog, Europeana Professional, 13 November 2015, http://pro.europeana.eu/blogpost/the-missing-decades-the-20th-century-black-hole-in-europeana.

2   European Commission, Orphan Works, 7 June 2016, http://ec.europa.eu/internal_market/copyright/orphan_works/index_en.htm.

3   Wellcome Library, Copyright Clearance and Takedown, 2017, https://wellcomelibrary.org/about-this-site/copyright-clearance-and-takedown/.

4   Gov.UK, Extended Collective Licensing, 1 October 2014, www.gov.uk/government/publications/extended-collective-licensing.

5   Kiley, R. et al., Clearing Rights to Digitise Books Published in the 20 Century: a case study prepared by the Wellcome Library, the Authors' Licensing and

Collecting Society and the Publishers Licensing Society, June 2013, bit.ly/2al58g9.

6   Wellcome Library, London's Pulse: Medical Officer of Health reports 1848–1972, 2017, http://wellcomelibrary.org/moh/.

7   Wellcome Library, *Access to Personal Data Within Our Research Collections*, 2014, http://wellcomelibrary.org/content/documents/policy-documents/access-to-personal-data.pdf.

8   See Gov.UK, Reducing the Duration of Copyright in Certain Unpublished Works, Intellectual Property Office, 31 October 2014, www.gov.uk/government/consultations/reducing-the-duration-of-copyright-in-certain-unpublished-works.

9   Stobo, V., Deazley, R. and Anderson, I. G., *Copyright & Risk: scoping the Wellcome Digital Library Project*, 2013, zenodo.org/record/8380/files/CREATe-Working-Paper-2013-10.pdf.

Chapter 11

Developing an open educational resources policy and open approaches to mitigate risk at University of Edinburgh

Melissa Highton, Assistant Principal, Online Learning, University of Edinburgh

> There is a risk to not being open, and not being open now will cost us money in the future.

This case study describes how the University of Edinburgh plans its approach to open educational resources in support of learning and teaching and offers suggestions to others working to make open educational resources sustainable in higher education institutions. It offers a clear value proposition for aligning open educational resources activities within institutional budgets and strategies for learning, teaching and research in the context of a digital university. Many cultural institutions making the move towards open practice struggle with the challenges of securing high-level 'buy-in' to support such initiatives; this case study also considers the institutional risks of 'open washing' and neglecting staff development in this area.

The University of Edinburgh leads the Scottish higher education sector in having a published open educational resources policy in place and a central service to support staff development in using open educational resources for learning and teaching. The University promotes and incentivises open educational practice in a range of ways through course design, institutional infrastructure and open knowledge partnerships, including hosting a Wikimedian in Residence to embed open practices inside and outwith the curriculum.

The University of Edinburgh context

Discussion started about an open educational resources policy for the University of Edinburgh in 2014. A high-level task group was established, including key opinion shapers from around the University and the Student Association (EUSA). The task group aimed to explore how high quality learning materials could be made open, not only for students within the University, but across Scotland and to the wider world.

At the time the University was riding the wave of global interest in massive open online courses (MOOCs) and in the light of the upcoming independence referendum many in Scotland saw a strategic opportunity to contribute to a fairer society via open educational practice. The resulting open educational resources vision for the University of Edinburgh has three strands designed to help learning technologists and academic colleagues decide which materials to release and where. The University of Edinburgh open educational resources policy was published to deliver the vision in 2016 and to support colleagues in making positive decisions for open practice.

The open educational resources vision for higher education

The University of Edinburgh's mission is to create, disseminate and curate knowledge, and our aim is to make a significant, sustainable and socially responsible contribution to Scotland. The three strands of the open educational resources vision build on our history of excellent education, research collections, the Scottish enlightenment and civic mission. This vision not only builds on work, custom and practice already in place within the University but offers an opportunity to take a strategic approach to deliver digital education by publishing open educational resources at scale.

The three strands of the University's open educational resources practice are described below; each is supported by specific strategic actions to ensure delivery.

For the common good

The University's open educational resources vision for the common good is:

- exchanging and sharing teaching and learning materials to enrich the University and the sector
- putting in place the support frameworks to enable any member of the University to publish and share online as open educational resources teaching and learning materials they have created as a routine part of their work at the University
- supporting students, researchers and staff to find and use high quality teaching materials developed within and outwith the University.

Edinburgh at its best

At its best, the University's open educational resources vision for Edinburgh is:

- showcasing openly the highest quality learning and teaching
- identifying collections of high quality learning materials within each school, department and research institute to be published online for flexible use, to be made available to learners and teachers as open courseware
- enabling the discovery of these materials in a way that ensures that the university's reputation is enhanced.

The university's treasures

The open educational resources vision for the University's treasures is:

- making available online to Scotland, the UK and the world a significant collection of unique learning materials that promotes health and economic and cultural well-being
- identifying a number of major collections of interdisciplinary materials, archives, treasures, and museum resources to be digitised, curated and shared for the greater good and significant contribution to public engagement with learning, study and research
- putting in place policy and infrastructure to ensure that these open educational resources collections are sustainable and usable in the medium to longer term.

Institutional infrastructure for sustainable open educational resources

At the University, open educational resources practice and policy is part of the infrastructure for an institution hoping to use its collections and content in myriad ways. Establishing a clear vision mitigates the reputational risk of colleagues referring to online learning materials as 'open' when they are available under a closed or unclear licence. The establishment of a central support service lessens the risk that colleagues are unclear about the decisions they should make about licensing, sharing and using online materials. With online education activity of such scale and diversity across the institution the value proposition for open licensing needs to be clear. For this reason the open educational resources activity within the University focuses on licensing content for reuse.

From an individual's perspective, a digital resource might only be used by them once, whereas the resource itself may have been used many times before by others and it is unlikely that a digital resource available online will only ever be used once by one person in one context. The principles underpinning the open educational resources vision are based on the hope that the more we remove barriers to access, the more open a 'thing' becomes. The more open a thing is, the more it will be used. The more a thing is used the more interesting things will happen as a result, and the more value it has as an open knowledge asset in our community.

With rapidly changing technology the formats used for creating learning materials quickly become obsolete. Without clear permission to make adaptations it is hard for legacy learning materials to be converted to new formats. From an institutional perspective, the more open the licence, the more sustainable the asset is, because it gives colleagues within the institution licence to make changes and updates, convert formats, save it, develop against it, move around, publish it again in new ways. In this way the open educational resources policy serves as essential infrastructure that underpins the business of teaching, learning, research and knowledge transfer at an enterprise level.

The University of Edinburgh approach to open educational resources is based on making assets sustainable at an institutional level, and for the process of doing that to become mainstreamed and sustainable. We aim to transform ways of working to lower the barrier to participation in open educational resources production as much as possible. This requires that the institutional learning technologists and academics must work together with University lawyers and librarians to establish simple workflows to release 'stuff' at scale, whether newly digitised resources or new, born-digital materials. A positive approach to open educational resources ensures that the central IT service teams proactively put systems and workflows in place which privilege open practice to support online and blended learning. A new approach to thinking about the long-term risks of closed or unclear licensing ensures that recurrent funding is available to support the activity and a positive approach to staff development and training ensures that colleagues are able to make informed choices.

Copyright debt: a new approach to open educational resources

In 2016, in order to gain support and ongoing investment for open educational resources practice, the University's central learning technology teams successfully pitched business cases to senior IT budget holders based on a new concept of 'copyright debt'. The concept of 'technical debt' is well understood by IT directors and university chief information officers. Technical debt is a metaphor often used in IT to explain why it costs so much to replace and maintain IT systems. Technical debt can be seen as the cost of not doing something properly in the first place. From the moment suppliers and service managers build a system poorly, without due attention to software code rigour and process, they begin to accrue debt and then interest on that debt. From the moment they do not fix, patch and maintain the code, the same thing happens. At some point the technical teams have to go back and fix or replace it, and the longer it is left the more expensive it will be. It is the software development equivalent of the old adage 'a stitch in time saves nine'.

'Copyright debt', this new way of thinking about open educational resources as institutional assets, drew similarities between 'technical debt' and the likely future costs of 'copyright debt' to gain support for recurrent funding of support services.

When making a value proposition for open educational resources we must think about the institutional risks of not being open. Institutional risks are sometimes legal, sometimes reputational, sometimes financial. In practice, IT directors work to mitigate risks early on, and avoid risks in the future. When there is a risk to not being open, not being open will cost us money in the future.

Generally, the risks of not engaging with open practice are reputational: other institutions are doing it; we might miss out on this good thing; we should be seen to be bold in digital education and leading edge in our open research.

There is also a risk to our reputation if colleagues do not seem to be up to date on licensing or copyright in e-learning, and refer to online materials or data as 'open' when they are not. Most of those risks are easily hidden under a smear of 'open washing' and vagueness about the definition of open in different contexts. These are not risks that normally convince senior management to invest, however. To convince an IT director or a chief information officer to invest in systems that have built-in open licensing workflows, protecting the institution against the risk of expensive copyright debt is proactive forward thinking.

Copyright debt begins to accrue to learning materials from the moment a colleague tells you that they do not have time to worry about the copyright licensing and metadata on their teaching materials and then load them up into a virtual learning environment (VLE), course management system, online course environment, digital learning platform or departmental website.

When open content licensing is not planned into workflows from the start, new content management systems begin to make a problem for reuse later. Many university systems, particularly those which are several years old, do not include a check box or require a copyright statement before uploading materials. If this is not required of the user at the time of deposit, the checking and metadata have to be reverse engineered later. Someone has to go back to those materials at some point to check them, figure out who made them and when, and check for third party content. The longer time passes (or the greater the staff change) between the original materials being uploaded into the system the harder it is to find the original source.

The cost becomes an issue for the business when the institution migrates from one VLE to another, from one website to another, or from one media asset management system to another. When any of these migrations occur lecturers and departmental administrators are asked to confirm that they have copyright permission for the materials they are migrating. Many will say that they do not know or remember, or do not have time to make corrections. They will suggest that someone in a central service (usually the library) should do the checking, and that is where the cost hits.

It is unlikely that the library is staffed to provide this service. Although many university libraries have copyright experts in their professional teams, their expertise is expensive and often specific to research or journal publication. An organisation would have to pay additional staff to check thousands of hours of teaching materials, and this is part of the potential cost of this open educational resources copyright debt. Without careful checking most of the materials will be discarded, colleagues will be disappointed that they have to make it all again, and enthusiasm for digital education may wane. This is an inherent risk to gaining support for blended learning and online learning practice in many disciplines.

The challenge in all this is that the individual academics making the materials are not alert to the longer term cost to the central services of this debt. The risk of copyright debt is not normally one that persuades busy individuals to take the time to change their practice, so it makes sense to build rigour for open practice into the workflows of enterprise-wide systems and services they use as soon as we possibly can. Making it easy for colleagues to make positive choices from the start should be part of our service.

As institutions it is also important that we include the requirements for proactive open licensing in the criteria we use to select new products from IT suppliers. We should ask vendors challenging questions on how their software and services will support our business need for open educational resources. Leadership in open educational resources practice requires a commitment from senior management and major institutions to policy, practice and vision for the benefit of the sector. The pragmatic partnerships we enter into with suppliers may reflect our position with regard to them. As we enter an age of global digital education at scale major cultural institutions that are knowledge providers with resource collections must think proactively about the role we play in sharing for reuse.

Supporting open practice

In addition to investment in digital systems, workflows and services the University of Edinburgh underpins its commitment to open educational resources practice with a range of staff development initiatives designed to support colleagues in gaining the knowledge they need to make informed licensing decisions, the digital skills they need for creating materials, and the understanding of how knowledge and content can be shared, used and contested online.

One of the first actions was to create a website (open.ed.ac.uk) to list and showcase open educational resources activities. During 2016–17 the University's open education team ran numerous staff development events, produced online guides to support practice, and contributed to formal programmes of academic staff development offered to new and existing staff. Information about these and upcoming initiatives can be found on the website (http://open.ed.ac.uk/about/), where materials are showcased (Figure 11.1 on the next page). The University's second action was to employ a Wikimedian in Residence to raise the profile of open knowledge projects such as Wikipedia, Wikimedia Commons, Wikidata, Wikisource and Wikibooks among our academic and researcher community. The residency project in partnership with Wikimedia UK resulted in the development of digital skills training sessions for staff and students to support their engagement with open knowledge practice and sharing. Many colleagues were first introduced to a critical view of open licensing and open sharing within their discipline domain through their engagement with Wikipedia edit-a-thons and Wikidata events. The relatively small cost of employing and hosting the Wikimedian in Residence has resulted in significant value in widespread discussion within the University and about digitisation, knowledge curation, research impact, public engagement and community participation by higher education institutions.

Conclusions

The experience of developing a high-level open educational resources strategy

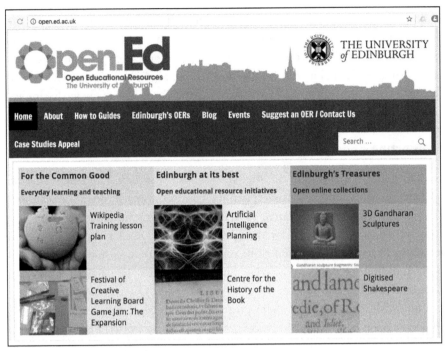

Figure 11.1 *The Open.Ed website*
Source: open.ed.ac.uk by University of Edinburgh licensed under a Creative Commons Attribution 4.0 International License

and vision for a large university committed to digital education and open knowledge practice at scale has required new thinking about the business case and financial models underpinning not only collections and resource management but also key digital learning systems, staff development and course materials production. By aligning open educational practice to institutional missions and investment, open educational resources activity, which might be seen by many as peripheral, can be brought into the centre of the infrastructure and services needed for growth and sustainability. The University of Edinburgh's planning, partnerships and practice have ensured that colleagues have a raised awareness of the importance of licensing and copyright in their teaching and learning activity and support to make enlightened decisions.

As higher education institutions endeavour to be successful in global digital platforms and differentiate themselves in that environment a commitment to open educational resources can be seen as a clear value proposition for success.

Chapter 12

How to implement open licensing

Introduction

The previous chapters and case studies have explained and demonstrated the need for, and benefits and challenges of, using open licences. We hope you are now convinced that open licensing is a viable proposition for encouraging the use and reuse of your organisation's resources. In this chapter we will take you through the steps necessary to implement open licensing: making the case to your senior managers, developing a policy and implementing it, and creating a sustainable open licensing environment.

How to make the case for open licensing

This first section explains how to begin the licensing process for organisations that have no established approach to licensing, open or otherwise. This is not only about making the case for open licensing, but above all about understanding your need for licensing, your licensing goals, and your organisation's willingness and appetite to engage with open licences in order to reach those goals. There are five steps involved in this process:

- Clarify your context.
- Obtain senior management buy-in.
- Express your vision and goals.
- Outline relevant licensing options.
- Document the decision.

Clarify your context

This step establishes context by surveying and noting the parameters that directly influence your decision to adopt an open licensing policy. As a first step to establishing any form of licensing approach or policy, open or otherwise, it is vital to identify, understand and capture your context. For open licensing by cultural heritage organisations, this most likely involves surveying and noting:

- the types of licensable material you have, especially identifying complex forms of material
- your user profile
- your organisational profile and strategy
- external limitations.

Identify types of licensable material

You need primarily to understand the types of licensable material your organisation has. All cultural heritage organisations have licensable material of one form or another. Establish how much licensable material your organisation has in broad terms. It is not necessary to develop a precise count of the number of licensable objects you hold. Rather, you should attempt to understand the types of licensable material your organisation holds and where within your organisational structure this material is located and cared for.

In general, most cultural heritage organisations have the following types of licensable material:

- digitised collection objects, including two-dimensional and three-dimensional works (e.g. digitised works of art, books, photographs and maps)
- surrogate collection objects in other, non-digital formats (e.g. film formats or microformats such as microfilms and microfiche)
- metadata (e.g. descriptive metadata)
- non-collection material (including policy documents and research data or outputs).

In this first step you are effectively taking an audit of your organisation's licensable material, which is subject to particular rights (e.g. copyright or database right) that enable the owner of those rights to allow other parties to use and reuse the material under specific conditions (see Chapter 3 for more information on copyright and licences).

This audit need not be complex or detailed. The aim is to identify which of the above broad categories of material you have that may be licensable – and at this stage you do not yet need to concern yourself with whether or how you may license them, that comes later. It will be beneficial to dig a bit deeper, in order to identify some specifics about the material, but it is not necessary to take a full audit and list every type of data you hold, or otherwise engross yourself in information gathering. As we discuss later, you may choose to license certain 'crown jewel' material uniquely, but by and large try to develop a systematic approach to licensing that can be broadly applied, as you would do with item description, for example.

Digging a bit deeper, you want at this stage to establish:

- whether you have material that is likely to require complex, multi-layer licensing, for example because the material has been jointly created by a number of parties (such as multi-authored works, films, videos or audio recordings)
- if you do not currently have licensable material in one of the above categories, whether you are likely to in the near future (e.g. if you are about to begin a programme of digitisation or 3D scanning).

The user profile of your organisation

As well as capturing broad, informative data about your licensable material, this is a good opportunity to note your organisation's user profile. Who are your users? For example, if you work in a university library you may have a clearly defined core audience of students and staff most likely to use your organisation's resources for coursework, research and academic publishing. On the other hand, if you work for a large national art museum your audience will likely be more diverse and their use of your resources will be similarly varied. Their use may encompass personal use, social media use, creative repurposing, publishing, and so on.

This can be tricky, and it is important not to become bogged down. Again, the information gathered at this stage should be light touch. Note user profiles, even if they are broad or loosely defined.

Organisational profile and strategy

Similarly, this stage is a good opportunity to refer back to your organisational profile and strategy. Again, this should not be an extensive exercise. As you are likely to have a fairly robust insight into your organisation – the way in which it operates, its mission, how it is funded, its key stakeholders, strategic vision and plans – this step may involve little work. Rather, it is important simply to ensure that you keep in mind the profile of your organisation, and keep efforts to develop open licensing in tune with your organisation's broader mission. Questions you might ask yourself include: What is my organisation specifically aiming to achieve? How will licensing, and in particular open licensing, serve (or fail to serve) these objectives? How does my licensable material fit within my organisation's wider strategic objectives? Are these materials directly referred to in the strategy?

External limitations

Finally, and significantly, during this initial stage it is important to note key external limitations that will have an impact on your licensing work. Obvious limitations include your sources of income and funding. Other key limitations to consider are the regulatory, organisational and legal specifications that structure your organisation. In particular, confirm that your organisation, or the work of your organisation, does not fall under the licensing policy remit of a parent body or structure. For example, if your organisation is a Crown copyright body in the UK[1] you normally need to comply with the UK Government Licensing Framework.[2] The exception is if your body has delegation of authority from Her Majesty's Stationery Office. For example, the British Film Institute and the Government Art Collection have delegations of authority for some licensable material. Organisations with delegations of authority are subject to the Information Fair Trader Scheme.[3]

Similarly, you should consider the licensing requirements of any of your subsidiary or related bodies, if you have any (e.g. a trading arm). The policies of these linked bodies may be beyond your control, but you should be clear and certain at this stage which body controls what material. In other words, do you know what licensable material is yours to license and what licensable material is your linked body's responsibility? Do you have jointly licensable material?

Having gathered together, or at least kept a watchful eye on this range of information, you should now have a reasonable understanding of your licensing context. You should have a view as to what types of licensable material you hold and whether any of that material will be particularly complex to license. You will have noted these materials in reference to the general profile of your users and organisation. Lastly, you will have taken into account your current strategic vision and the particular and key external limitations that are likely to play a part in your licensing work further down the line. With this information you should be in a position to begin raising awareness within your organisation, specifically with senior management, about the need for an organisational approach to, or policy on, licensing.

Obtain a mandate

The aims of this step are to outline to senior management why your organisation needs to develop an approach to licensing, to outline the broad types of licensable material your organisation has, and to obtain a mandate (or senior management buy-in) to produce a series of licensing options.

As with all strategic processes, obtaining and maintaining a mandate, likely instigated or supported by senior management buy-in, is critical throughout the development and implementation of an open licensing policy or approach. This is true irrespective of whether your approach to open licensing implementation is top down or bottom up, or a combination thereof.[4]

At this initial stage, engagement with senior management should be high level and introductory. You are attempting to raise awareness of the need for licensing, primarily by outlining the types of licensable material your organisation has. This is unlikely to be the time to present senior management with licensing options. Instead, seek from them a mandate to generate options for pursuing the use of licences for your material.

A simple method to achieve this step may be to present your senior management with a short briefing paper. Outline, at a high level, the types of licensable material your organisation has, for example collection materials, documents and metadata, and provide a few examples in order to make clear the scope and variety within the material. If your organisation routinely generates detailed and discursive descriptions of items, for example, it may be valuable to flag this to senior management at this stage as an example of the detail and variety found within your metadata. Along with a brief outline, use this opportunity to remind senior management of the benefits and risks of licensing, and the risks and benefits of leaving licensable material unlicensed.

Finally, use this as a chance to note if your organisation has any particularly complex licensable material, such as content jointly generated by numerous parties or under complex agreements, and whether your organisation is likely in the near future to produce other types of licensable material, such as three-dimensional scans, not currently being managed. Conclude your briefing with a request that senior management provides its support to the development of an organisational approach to licensing, or to the development of a licensing policy.

This will serve as your mandate to produce an options paper, and early buy-in from senior staff will be key at later stages when implementing open licences.

Express your vision and goals

This step combines the data gathered when you clarified your context, the mandate (and any steer) obtained when seeking consent from senior management, and your organisation's mission and ethos in order to identify a vision and set of goals for your use of open licences.

This is the 'big thinking' and ambition stage: what can open licences do for your organisation and its licensable material? How will you achieve that vision? In particular, at this stage you should attempt to align the benefits of licensing and of openness (as outlined in chapters 3 and 4) with your organisation's specific context. Set a high-level vision, for example:

- 'We will operate a clear, transparent, and sustainable licensing policy.'
- 'Our approach to licensing will ensure maximum benefit to users and reusers.'
- 'Our organisation's licensing policy will maximise access while protecting vital sources of income.'
- 'Our licensing policy will be optimised for access while protecting third party intellectual property rights.'

Support this vision with an initial set of quantifiable and realistic goals. At this early stage these goals are unlikely to be 'end goals', but even small-step goals that set your work in the right direction, towards your vision, will be of benefit. For example, you might set the following goals:

- 'By the end of Year 1, we will have produced new written licensing guidance for staff and a refreshed licensing information web page for users.'
- 'By the end of Year 2 we will have identified and applied appropriate licences or rights statements to at least 95% of our digitised works.'
- 'By the end of Year 2 we will have openly licensed all our own metadata and identified all metadata that contains third party intellectual property rights.'
- 'By the time 50% of our digitised collections are published with open licences, we will have increased visits to our digital collections by 15% compared to year zero.'
- 'We will monitor and report annually to senior management on the impact

of licensed resources against our existing income generation targets.'
- 'We will promote our licensed resources through regular updates on our existing social media channels to encourage use and reuse.'

Outline relevant licensing options

The aims of this step are to act on your mandate by translating your requirements, vision and goals into a concise options appraisal of the three broad licensing options: open, semi-closed and closed.

Once you have established your organisation's licensing requirements, obtained a mandate, and understood your vision and initial goals, the final step in making the case for open licences is to outline a set of licensing options for senior management.

One way to structure this options appraisal is to think first of the three broad types of licences we outlined in this book: open, semi-closed and closed. You may decide that your ideal licensing approach combines two or even three of these. Such a 'mixed' approach to licensing may be entirely rational and appropriate, particularly with cultural heritage organisations dealing in a wide range of licensable material, such as numerous types of metadata, several varieties of digitised content, and a range of non-collection material.

For example, a cultural heritage organisation that handles a wide range of licensable metadata, content and non-collection material may opt for a diversified licensing approach that combines a number of open licences for metadata and some collection material, semi-closed licences for other collection material and most non-collection material, and a closed approach to a limited range of non-collection material.

If possible outline to your senior management various possible licensing approaches, providing for each approach:

- a description (e.g. an explanation of the licences that it uses)
- a justification showing how it fits with institutional requirements and vision
- an explanation of its benefits
- a summary of its risks.

Table 12.1 on the next page compares two types of licences as an example of a possible licensing approach.

Table 12.1 *Example of a licensing proposal to senior management*

	CC BY	CC BY-NC-SA
Description	All digitised copies created by the organisation, where the originating work is in the public domain All metadata created by the organisation All documents for public consumption	All digitised copies created by the organisation, where the originating work is a 'valued collection asset' where the organisation wants actively to control commercial reuse
How this approach fits with institutional requirements and vision	Provides access to our collections Promotes knowledge and understanding Encourages learning and research	Provides access to our collections Promotes knowledge and understanding Encourages learning and research
Benefits	Maximises use and impact Satisfies strategic objectives	Maximises use and impact for non-commercial purposes Enables the organisation to control commercial use and reuse Satisfies strategic objectives
Risks	May limit use owing to attribution requirement Users of such content may ignore attribution requirement May impact potential for income generation	May limit use owing to non-commercial requirement Users of such content may ignore the non-commercial requirement

Document the decision

Assuming your senior management team approves the vision for open licensing and the proposed licensing approach, the final step before implementation is to document and formalise this decision. This is important for two reasons:

- your organisation will be altering its approach to managing the intellectual property rights status of its resources, and as a result there should be a documented audit trail of this decision
- the licensing options must be clearly and explicitly documented, as this documentation will be used by you and your colleagues when open licences are being assigned to resources.

You may find it useful to write a short policy document, which outlines the open licences agreed.

The work of implementing open licensing

The aims of this step are to develop a plan to implement your licensing policy; put in place procedures and documentation that support the policy and enable licences to be applied to your resources; communicate the policy to staff and promote it to your users; and gather metrics, report back and review your policy.

With a mandate to openly license your organisation's resources and the licensing approach documented and agreed, it is time to get down to the work of implementation. As discussed, a number of the benefits of open licensing revolve around the generation of efficiency and practicality, and for these benefits to be realised it is essential that the process of licensing is integrated into the organisational workflow. There are several interrelated components that ensure your organisation has a sustainable licensing environment:

- audit resources
- determine if a given resource can be openly licensed
- record and store information gathered during the licensing process
- communicate with users about the licence
- communicate with staff
- review the licensing
- monitor compliance and usage
- advocate for the policy, process and benefits.

Audit resources

If you already undertook a lightweight audit of your organisation's licensable material, as we suggested earlier in the chapter, then you are in a good position to start the process of applying licences. If you did not complete an audit, then now is the time to do so (see section 'Identify types of licensable material section', page 165). As mentioned, this audit should not be detailed – it is more to get a feel for the range, categories and complexities of the material that you may want to license. Your audit will likely reveal a range of potentially licensable materials, for example:

- digitised collections where the original work is in the public domain
- digitised collections where the original work is in-copyright and/or has multiple rights holders
- organisational documents where your organisation holds all copyright

- organisational documents where your organisation holds the copyright in the text but the images are copyright of a photographer
- descriptive metadata created within your organisation
- descriptive metadata which is partially or wholly licensed from third parties.

Your audit should also consider what materials and resources will likely require licensing in the future. Perhaps you are planning the three-dimensional digitisation of sculpture, or a website featuring a previously unseen collection of correspondence between two 20th-century poets, or your organisation's forthcoming annual report.

Just before you start to determine the appropriate licence (see section 'Determine the licence', below) for a resource or a collection of resources, it is worth quickly spot-checking to confirm that your assumptions about the materials are accurate. For example, if materials are in-copyright and the copyright holder has given you permission to digitise them and make them available under an open licence, it will be useful to check that there are not any further, unaccounted-for third party copyright holders in the works.

Determine the licence

The aim at this stage is to document the process by which a resource is examined in order to determine what licence may be assigned. Ideally, the procedure should be clear and easy to use, taking users through the complete process. A useful approach is to be pragmatic and ask a series of questions about the resource, the answers to which will ultimately determine its licence. These are the most basic questions to ask:

- Who holds the intellectual property rights associated with this resource?
- Is this resource a (digital) representation of another resource? If so, is that underlying resource in the public domain? If not, who holds the intellectual property rights to the underlying resource?
- Is this resource currently licensed; if so, what is its licence?
- Does our licensing policy have any exceptions that might prevent or restrict the licensing of this resource? If not, what licence does the policy state should be applied?

Let's take a hypothetical example of several albums of Victorian photographic prints that your organisation has purchased, and subsequently created digitised versions of, with the intention of making them available on your website. In this instance, the resources that we are considering for licensing are the digital images of the photographs, not the original photographs themselves.

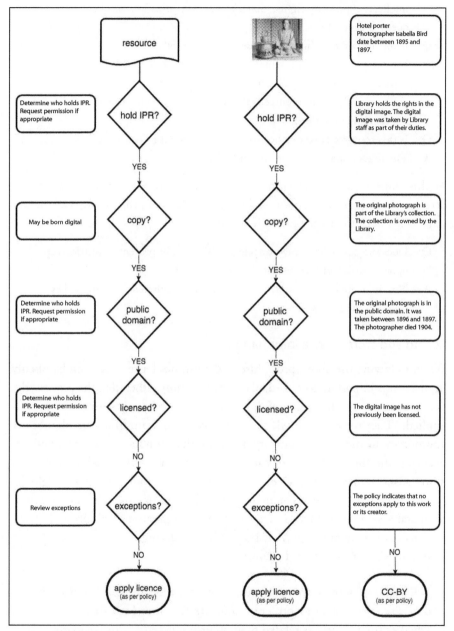

Figure 12.1 *Example of a workflow to determine a licence (CC BY)*
   Source: Gill Hamilton and Fred Saunderson, National Library of Scotland

Q   Who holds the intellectual property rights associated with this resource?

A   My organisation created the digital images and therefore holds any intellectual property rights. Given this my organization may be able to openly license this resource.

Q   Is this resource a (digital) representation of another resource?

A   Yes, this is a digital representation of another resource.

Q   If so, is that underlying resource in the public domain?

A   Yes, that underlying resource is the public domain – the original photographer died in 1904.

Q   Is this resource currently licensed, and if so, what is its licence?

A   The digital images are not currently licensed.

At this stage it is safe to assume that you may openly license these images because your organisation alone holds any intellectual property rights. The last stage is to check the policy for exclusions:

Q   Does the policy have any exceptions which might prevent or restrict the open licensing of this resource?

A   No, there are no restrictions and the licence can therefore be applied as stated in the policy.

Record and store licence information

When following the above procedure to determine if a resource can be openly licensed, it is important to record all the information gathered in the process, the decision taken on licensing and, where appropriate, the licence that was applied. The method by which you record this information should be appropriate to the size of your organisation, the number of resources you are licensing and the complexity of your licensing regime. For a small organisation a spreadsheet may be sufficient. For larger organisations the data might be recorded in an asset management system such as a library catalogue, collection or digital asset management system. However, for greatest flexibility and utility, a rights management system may be worth considering.

At a minimum you should record:

- a description of the resource including its identifier (e.g. an ID in a database, a persistent identifier or Uniform Resource Identifier)
- whether the resource is related to another resource (e.g. an analogue original)

- who holds the intellectual property rights in the resource and any related resources
- what licence was applied.

It is not necessary to itemise each individual resource in your spreadsheet or asset or rights management database. You can describe common resources at a collection level. If we return to our example of the digitised versions of the Victorian photographic prints, if you know the remaining underlying photographs in the collection were taken by the same photographer under the same general conditions and that the remaining digital representations were also created under comparable conditions (e.g. none were separately created by a third party), it is safe to assume that the associated images will have the same licence outcome as the image you walked through the licensing process already. Therefore the whole collection of digital images can be recorded as a single entry in your licence recording system. Take care as not all collections will be this straightforward. For example, if the underlying photographs were in fact a collection of works created by a variety of photographers, it may not be safe to assume that they are all out-of-copyright. In such cases you may need to record licensing information at a lower level of detail, for example image by image.

Below is a list of elements and data points that you may want to consider recording. Those marked with * indicate the fields that should be considered mandatory. Elements and data points to record about the resource being licensed include:

- a short description or a link or persistent identifier to its description in another database*
- its public location, such as its URL on your website
- its date of creation; record if the date is not known
- the intellectual property rights holder;* record if the rights holder is not known
- any contractual or regulatory information that applies to the resource; record if there is none.

These are some elements and data points to record about related resources:

- a description about related resources, such as the resource from which digital copies are made
- its date of creation; record if the date is not known

- its location within your organisation or wherever it resides (e.g. a shelf mark)
- the intellectual property rights holder, if known;* record if the rights holder is not known
- any licence, contractual or regulatory information that applies to the resource; record if there is none.

These are some elements and data points to record about the licence:

- whether an open licence was applied or not*
- if so, the date the licence was applied*
- if so, the version or date of the policy that was consulted for licensing*
- if no licence was applied, why*.

Figures 12.2–12.5 give examples of how resources and licence data may be recorded.

Resource: Forth Bridge illustrations, 1886–7	
Description	Forth Bridge illustrations 1886–7
Type	collection of resources
Number of parts	44 images
Format	digital copy of analogue work
Identifier	DOD:74570306
Identifier type	persistent, collection level
Published location	http://digital.nls.uk/74570306
Location type	persistent
Creation date	2005/04/06
Creation date type	exact
Intellectual property rights holder	National Library of Scotland
Intellectual property rights holder status	active
Related resources	
Identifier	3748284
Identifier type	non-persistent, bibliographic record identifier
Type	analogue original
Creation date	1887/01/01
Creation date type	circa
Intellectual property rights holder	Philip Phillips
Intellectual property rights holder status	inactive

Figure 12.2 *Continued*

Under licence, contract	no
Licence	
Licence applied	YES
Licence	CC BY
Policy version	2016/04/01
Licence decision	original in public domain
Licence note	none

Figure 12.2 *Resource and licence data on a collection of digital images originating from Victorian photographs*

Resource: Scotia Depicta	
Description	Scotia Depicta
Type	1 single item
Number of parts	104 images
Format	digital copy of analogue work
Identifier	DOD:74582230
Identifier type	persistent, title level
Published location	http://digital.nls.uk/74465058
Location type	persistent
Creation date	2013/09/06
Creation date type	approximate
Intellectual property rights holder	National Library of Scotland
Intellectual property rights holder status	active
Related resources	
Identifier	J.134.f
Identifier type	non-persistent, book shelfmark
Type	analogue original
Creation date	1804/01/01
Creation date type	approximate
Intellectual property rights holder	National Library of Scotland
Intellectual property rights holder status	active
Licence	
Licence applied	CC BY
Policy version	2016/04/01
Licence decision	original in public domain
Licence note	none

Figure 12.3 *Resource and licence data on a collection of images that represent a digitised book*

Resource: Takedown policy	
Description	Takedown policy
Type	1 single item
Number of parts	1 PDF
Format	born-digital, corporate document
Identifier	none
Identifier type	not applicable
Published location	http://www.nls.uk/media/1253511/takedown-policy-2016.pdf
Location type	non-persistent
Creation date	2016/08/06
Creation date type	exact
Intellectual property rights holder	National Library of Scotland
Intellectual property rights holder status	active
Related resources	
Identifier	none
Identifier type	not applicable
Type	not applicable
Creation date	not applicable
Creation date type	not applicable
Intellectual property rights holder	not applicable
Intellectual property rights holder status	not applicable
Licence	
Licence applied	CC BY
Policy version	2016/04/01
Licence decision	corporate document, non-confidential
Licence note	none

Figure 12.4 *Resource and licence data on a digital document relating to the business of an organisation*

Resource: Discover: the magazine of National Library of Scotland	
Description	Discover: the magazine of National Library of Scotland
Type	continuing publication (serial)
Number of parts	multiple
Format	born-digital, corporate document
Identifier	none
Identifier type	not applicable
Published location	http://www.nls.uk/about-us/publications/discover
Location type	non-persistent
Creation date	2012

Figure 12.5 *Continued*

Creation date type	circa
Intellectual property rights holder	National Library of Scotland
Intellectual property rights holder status	active
Intellectual property rights holder	advertisers (multiple)
Intellectual property rights holder status	active
Intellectual property rights holder	contributors (multiple)
Intellectual property rights holder status	active
Related resources	
Identifier	none
Identifier type	not applicable
Type	not applicable
Creation date	not applicable
Creation date type	not applicable
Intellectual property rights holder	not applicable
Intellectual property rights holder status	not applicable
Licence	
Licence applied	Copyright all rights reserved National Library of Scotland, contributors and advertisers, unless otherwise stated
Policy version	2016/04/01
Licence decision	corporate document, non-confidential, multiple rights holders
Licence note	Copyright may lie with multiple rights holders including advertisers, illustrators, photographers, authors, etc

Figure 12.5 *Resource and licence data on an organisational magazine that contains third party copyright in text and images*

Communicate with users about the licence

One of the principal reasons to license cultural heritage resources openly is to encourage their use and reuse. It is therefore vital to communicate about open licences not only with your existing users but also with new and potential users. There are two key objectives to this communication:

- to raise awareness and promote your openly licensed resources
- to outline the practicalities of using and reusing such resources.

Raise awareness and promote the use and reuse of resources

Having developed and implemented your open licensing policy it is time to publicise the policy and promote the use and reuse of your resources.

Your organisation will likely have spent considerable time and effort developing its policy and applying open licences to resources. However, most of your users will probably have little interest in learning the background to and specifics of your policy as they are mainly interested in accessing and using the resources. To that end, you should not focus on publicising your policy directly. Instead, promote its benefits, and what the policy means for users, by promoting your resources.

We can look again at the example of the digitised Victorian photographic prints and their publication on your organisation's website (Figure 12.2). The collection can be highlighted via social media networks such as Twitter, Instagram and Facebook, and perhaps given more detail and background in a blog post on your website. Assuming this collection is of cultural and/or organisational significance, you might promote it further with a press release, articles in professional and academic publications, and events or talks. Through all of these communication methods give positive and encouraging messages, in non-technical terms, about how the digital images can be used and reused. For example, you could use social media to highlight the easy reusability of the material for fun and creative purposes, while at events or in papers you may want to focus on the ability for scholars to take the images and use them seamlessly and freely to make comparisons with other works from the same era.

Use and reuse practicalities

One of the main reasons to license cultural heritage resources openly is to encourage their use and reuse by anyone, and it is therefore important that information about how they might be used is clear, brief and avoids overly complex terminology.

Most likely you will be publishing your openly licensed resources on your organisation's website. You must make a brief statement about the licence of every licensed image or document and provide links to fuller information. For example, we can look one last time at our digitised Victorian photographs (Figure 12.6 opposite) and assume they are displayed gallery-style on a website, using thumbnails images. Somewhere on that gallery page, perhaps towards the bottom, there must be a brief statement about the licence that applies to the thumbnails. On selecting a thumbnail users are taken to detailed page about that particular image; there must be a brief statement about the licence on that page too. In both instances, it would be good practice to accompany the statement with a link to more detailed information. For example, the statement might read 'Creative Commons Attribution', 'CC BY' or 'public domain' and have a link to another page where more information is given about how the resource may be used.

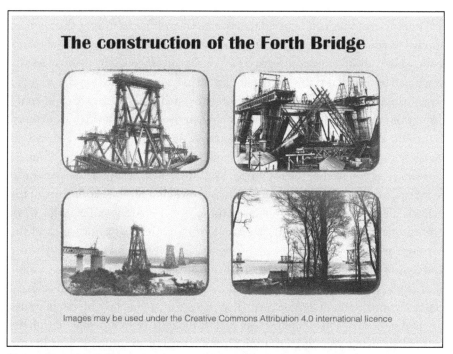

Figure 12.6 *Photos illustrating the construction of the Forth Bridge (CC BY)*
Source: Gill Hamilton, Fred Saunderson, National Library of Scotland

Figure 12.7 *Photo illustrating the construction of the Forth Bridge (CC BY)*
Source: Gill Hamilton, Fred Saunderson, National Library of Scotland

Other techniques can be used to assist users in understanding the licences applied to your resources. If you allow users to download images or documents from your website, you could create a pop-up message when they select the download option that states the licence associated with the file they are about to download. Similarly, if you allow printing or e-mailing of resources you could display or embed the licence information when the user selects these functions. You could also embed the licence information, along with other details such as ownership, in the image's technical metadata (XMP[5]) either at point of image creation or as you license the resources. Most users never examine this technical metadata, and the presence of the information will not inhibit routine use of the material. However, photographers, graphic designers and others who work professionally with digital imagery are familiar with this technology and the presence of such detail could be highly beneficial to them and their ability to use and reuse your content safely, and to provide attribution or a provenance trail.

It is good practice to develop an area of your website that explains clearly, concisely and without jargon your licensing policy and how users may use licensed resources. This should set out plainly the responsibilities that lie with the user when using your organisation's resources. For example, if you license resources with the CC BY-NC-SA licence you must explain that users need to attribute your organisation and not sell or generate income from the resources, and to do otherwise is to be in breach of the licence. It would also be helpful to users if you explained and supplied model examples of how your organisation expects to be attributed. You might also point them in the direction of best practice and tools such as Open Attribute Builder (see section 'Attribution resources and tools' in Chapter 13).[6]

Communicate with staff

Equally as important as communicating with users is communicating with staff at your organisation. Moving to an open licensing framework is usually a significant change and staff will need a clear understanding of the policy and the reasoning behind it. Those who are responsible for licensing need to be confident about how to use the licensing procedure and the information gathering and recording processes.

Once the policy is approved, but before implementation commences, staff need to be briefed. How this is best done will depend on the size of your organisation and number and range of staff that are responsible for licensing or advising on the licensing and reuse of resources. We suggest that you consider several means of communication from the following: simple e-mails, documentation, briefing sessions, short training workshops and drop-in sessions. Briefing sessions and workshops are particularly important for those who license resources and staff who engage or work with users. These events must explain why the organisation has adopted an open licensing approach and outline the benefits and risks as well as more of the practical details, such as how the organisation would like to be attributed. Those on the frontline, dealing with users' queries, need to understand the policy well enough to explain how resources may or may not be used.

Review the licensing

It is important to round off the implementation process by taking steps to keep your licensing under review. As with all intellectual property matters, and as likely with all policy matters in your organisation, open licences do not remain static forever. Plan reviews of your licences in advance, whether of your policy in general or of specific licences. If you have applied a particularly restrictive form of semi-open licence, such as a Creative Commons licence with a non-commercial or no-derivatives element, you should ensure that you plan a review of this restriction in advance. It may be that after a number of years this level of restriction is no longer warranted or necessary. Conscious planning for review at an early stage can help to avoid future gaps or uncertainties (e.g. see the section 'Copyright debt: a new approach to open educational resources' in the case study on the University of Edinburgh, Chapter 11).

Planned instances of review will help you to maintain an active level of monitoring over your resources (see section 'Monitor compliance and usage', below), and will also help you justify your licences over the longer term, optimising your use of the correct licence as situations change or as time progresses. As discussed, it is important to bear in mind that once an open licence has been applied to a work, it is legally and practically challenging or impossible to revert to a more restrictive licence. In this way, it is likely that your review processes will centre on attempting to assess your use of open licences to either maintain the status quo or move to more open licences, if possible. Be prepared to remove licences and mark materials as being in the public domain as rights expire.

Knowing that your policy and licence implementation will be reviewed may help when you are telling other stakeholders about the move to open licences. If necessary, a scheduled review stage can allow you to apply semi-open licences initially, such as a CC BY-NC-SA licence, rather than a fully open one, such as CC BY. In this manner you can use a planned review to allow your organisation to experiment with the opportunity to assess the impact of a semi-open licence and consider a future move to an open licence in due course.

When conducting a review, these are some of the things you may wish to consider:

- usage and access statistics, ideally across a range of channels; consider, for example, the access figures that the National Library of Wales was able to extract from resource use via Wikimedia Commons
- income and expenditure related to any non-open licensing (e.g. if you have been licensing CC BY-NC material separately for commercial reuse requests)
- engagement with open resources compared with closed or semi-closed resources
- impact on staff working time (e.g. you may want to examine whether staff are spending more or less time on handling licensing matters)
- impact on media, social media and other communication channels that could result from your move to open licences
- any complaints or queries from third party stakeholders (such as digitisation partners)
- any positive feedback from third parties.

Monitor compliance and usage

Once you have applied open licences to your material, you may need to ensure some degree of monitoring, particularly if you have placed restrictions on the degree of openness, such as commercial use or derivative restrictions. Depending on how you make the material available, it may be extremely challenging or impossible for you to enforce restrictions effectively. For example, if you have released images online under a CC BY-NC-SA licence it may not be within your reasonable means to monitor whether images have been used commercially elsewhere. However, you may be able to monitor compliance with your licences to a certain extent, for example by watching out for use of the content in publications or in common open resource platforms, like Wikimedia Commons (see section 'Tools and resources' in Chapter 13 for tools that can assist in monitoring).

It may be practical to integrate any monitoring that you undertake with any established copyright and digital access monitoring processes you have. For example, if you run a takedown policy it may be practical to integrate a degree of licence monitoring into the takedown process, using any takedown requests as opportunities to check for potential licence transgressions in relation to that material.

Advocate for the policy, process and benefits

Throughout the implementation process it may be important to advocate for open licences. Looking back at your open licensing and digital *raisons d'être*, as well as the various benefits of openness and open licences set out in this book, it could be useful to remain proactive in espousing benefits and ensuring that stakeholders are comfortable with the process. This may at times be as simple as keeping stakeholders and colleagues informed about progress. Workshops or training sessions around your new licensing policy can be good opportunities to remind colleagues about why you are moving to open licences. Advocacy should not be propaganda, but instead about keeping up a positive message. Open licences can be a significant change for some collections, organisations or individuals, and at times the benefits may seem distant or opaque.

How to perfect the use of open licensing

Once embedded as part of your normal practices, an agreed approach to open licensing can be hugely beneficial. Earlier in this chapter we detailed practical and organisational processes that you may wish to undertake in order to make the case for, and then implement, an open licensing approach within your organisation. The aim of this section is to help you realise the benefits set out in Chapter 4 and in the case studies, as well as to benefit from lessons learned by early adopter organisations. These implementation processes aim to affirm the sustainable position of your open licensing policy and to attain business as usual with your functional open licensing activities. However, completion of these aims should not be perceived as the termination of efforts to benefit from an open approach.

Successfully making the case for, designing and implementing an open licensing approach should naturally be viewed as highly desirable, and a comfortable place to be. As business as usual, open licensing should become a practical, plausible and understood method of working for an organisation, following the process detailed above and taking the lessons from the preceding case studies. Organisations should have in place the policy and functional tools, as well as the organisational buy-in, to enable a more hands-off approach to open licensing. For example, when your digitisation teams create new image sets, they may now embed a CC BY licence for those images in the metadata as part of their publication workflow.

In order to maximise the benefits you will derive from openness, from processes of implementing open licences and, with all likelihood, from openness for your users and other stakeholders, we recommend that you engage in some longer term activities aimed at perfecting your use of open licences. In particular, we recommend that you begin work to:

- attend to any backlogs of unlicensed, closed material (or 'pre-open' material)
- promote your openness and communicate openly about your ongoing activities
- encourage concerted efforts to use and reuse open material – further embed yourself within the open ecosystem to which you are now contributing.[7]

Converting existing resources to the new policy

A rational way to avoid becoming bogged down in the details of legacy materials and past decisions is, initially at least, to implement open licensing with your new and current material, not your older legacy material. It is likely that your approach to licensing grew up in an ad hoc manner or involved a different approach from the one you have now adopted. By focusing on contemporary materials and activities at the start, you will be able to ensure momentum is maintained and that your policy and functional processes are aligned to your current and future activities, which is where they are most relevant.

That said, we do not advocate ignoring your legacy materials. Once your contemporary material and activities are benefiting from business as usual open licensing, you should turn your attention to your pre-existing resources and their review and conversion, where appropriate, to your new open licensing regime. It may be especially useful to commence this work quickly, in order to continue the momentum you have generated and sustained during the implementation processes above and to ensure that you maintain a consistent, coherent and accessible approach to licensing. By going back over your older materials you can help to communicate clear reuse permissions in relation to all of your material, not just your newest sets. Indeed, remixing older content and revising licensing positions can give a new lease of life and open content up for greater use and reuse.

In general your approach should be:

- to attempt, as far as possible, to review and record licensing decisions for all pre-existing materials regardless of whether you license them openly or not
- for pre-existing resources where no rights or licence statement exists, to resolve as far as possible to provide a statement to this effect with the resources

- to look for collections of pre-existing resources that yield quick open licensing wins and convert them to your new licensing framework as quickly as possible so as to maximise their impact, use and reuse
- to accept that there are likely to be pre-existing resources that do not warrant conversion to open licensing because of complexity with their rights, contractual, legal, privacy or related obligations.

If you have undertaken an audit (see earlier in this chapter) it will inform you of the size and complexity of the retro-conversion required, and help you decide what approaches may apply to relicensing your materials. From your audit you may see resources falling into different categories that help you prioritise your efforts for maximum impact. For example, perhaps your audit shows that there are many resources digitised from public domain works in which your organisation solely holds the intellectual property rights – such resources will likely be 'quick wins' and can readily be converted to new licences. Maybe your audit reveals that all published legacy corporate documents such as annual reports, plans, strategies and plans contain at least some copyrighted materials – then you might determine not to convert such documents to your open licensing policy retrospectively as this would place a significant burden on your organisation in identifying rights holders and clearing copyright without a corresponding benefit in use and reuse. Your audit may identify resources where there is no rights holder or licence information. These will likely be some of the most complex issues to address and resolve.

Notes

1   UK Crown copyright bodies are listed at The National Archives, Crown Copyright, n.d., www.nationalarchives.gov.uk/information-management/reusing-public-sector-information/uk-government-licensing-framework/crown-copyright/.

2   The National Archives, UK Government Licensing Framework, n.d., www.nationalarchives.gov.uk/information-management/reusing-public-sector-information/uk-government-licensing-framework/.

3   A full list is available at The National Archives, Delegations of Authority, n.d., www.nationalarchives.gov.uk/information-management/reusing-public-sector-information/uk-government-licensing-framework/crown-copyright/delegations-of-authority/.

4   See discussions of top-down, bottom-up and combined approaches to policy implementation in Cerna, L., *The Nature of Policy Change and Implementation: a*

review of different theoretical approaches, Organisation for Economic Co-Operation and Development, 2013, www.oecd.org/edu/ceri/The%20Nature%20of%20Policy%20Change%20and%20Implementation.pdf.

5   Adobe, XMP Specification Part 2: additional properties, 2016, http://wwwimages.adobe.com/content/dam/Adobe/en/devnet/xmp/pdfs/XMP%20SDK%20Release%20cc-2016-08/XMPSpecificationPart2.pdf.

6   Creative Commons, Best Practices for Attribution, 5 March 2014, https://wiki.creativecommons.org/wiki/Best_practices_for_attribution.

7   Heimstädt, M., Saunderson, F. and Heath, T., From Toddler to Teen: growth of an open data ecosystem, *Journal of eDemocracy and Open Government*, **6** (2), 2014, www.jedem.org/index.php/jedem/article/view/330.

Chapter 13

Using and reusing openly licensed resources

Introduction

This chapter describes what you, your colleagues and people who use your services and content need to know about using and reusing openly licensed resources. It also outlines a range of tools, techniques and services that can be used to help find and correctly attribute open content and explains how to distribute resources to third party services where they can reach more users and have greater impact.

Correct use of open resources

The internet is awash with an ever-increasing wealth of openly licensed resources, all of which is available to organisations to use and reuse for almost any purpose: there are images that can be used in presentations, posters and documents, texts and data to support research, courseware and videos to help train staff, operating systems and software applications to underpin business processes, and your organisation's own open content. By using open material you not only champion and support the open movement but are likely to save your organisation money, since open resources are generally free to use and repurpose.

It is important to make proper and correct use of openly licensed resources, and to ensure staff have at least a basic grasp of the obligations set out in open licences. Like your users, staff do not need to develop an in-depth knowledge of open licensing, but need enough of an understanding to use open resources correctly so as not to expose the organisation to the risks associated with misuse, inadvertent or otherwise.

Staff should be aware of the most common types of open licences that they are likely to encounter when sourcing resources for reuse. This requires explanation and documentation in plain and clear language about licensing frameworks, such as Creative Commons licences, the Open Government Licence and GNU licences. As Creative Commons is the open licensing framework most used in the cultural heritage sector it is worth going into more detail to explain the concepts of Attribution, ShareAlike, NonCommercial and NoDerivatives. Creative Commons Australia's colourful licensing fact sheet,[1] which is openly licensed itself (under a CC BY licence), could be a useful starting point and can be adapted to suit the needs of your organisation. Staff require a basic understanding of the public domain and the parameters of copyright duration for works in different formats and within different jurisdictions. The Copyright User website (http://copyrightuser.org/) offers useful guidance on the public domain in the UK and content on the site is available under a CC BY licence.[2]

To encourage correct use of open resources it may be useful to provide staff with examples of best practice of how to cite and attribute materials, and consider adopting a preferred style for attribution and require that all employees follow this guidance.

It is common for staff to forget to attribute their own organisation when reusing its open resources. This is, understandably, due to staff's familiarity with and proximity to their local resources, and perhaps because they do not realise or remember that these resources may be visible to others within and outwith their organisation. Staff should be reminded that attribution and licence compliance is always required regardless of whether the resource originates from within their own organisation or elsewhere. When local resources are correctly cited by staff it ensures that anyone else using them, whether another member of staff or someone outside the organisation, is aware of the licence terms.

Almost everyone who has used open resources will at one time or another not have complied completely with a licence, often as a result of forgetting to note the location of the resource and then being unable to find it again. Colleagues should be made aware that such non-compliance could lead to litigation against the organisation, cause reputational damage, and may result in charges of misconduct or dismissal against the employee. More fundamentally, regardless of whether these serious charges and consequences of non-compliance ever arise, staff should understand that it is good practice for a cultural heritage organisation to recognise and attribute the creators of creative works appropriately and to comply with licence terms correctly. It is therefore important to stress and encourage colleagues to adopt good habits when sourcing open resources, such as noting down the locations or URLs of resources so that they can be revisited later to confirm licence terms.

Finally, to encourage staff to use open resources in their work it may be helpful to show and explain tools and techniques for sourcing open content. The 'Tools and resources' section later in this chapter has a description of several useful services and repositories.

Advice for users of open resources

To encourage users to use, reuse and redistribute openly licensed resources correctly, it is important that resources include a licence statement and guidance that explains the licence.

The licence statement

Every resource that your organisation publishes, whether openly licensed or otherwise and regardless of whether it is published on your organisation's website, a third party website or offline, should carry with it a licence or rights statement. The licence statement should contain at least two basic components: the licence itself, for example 'CC BY', and what the licence refers to, for example 'this image'.

The following additional components that should be added to the licence statement include:

- hyperlinks or URLs directing users to the full text of the licence, for example providing a link to the licence on the Creative Commons website
- hyperlinks or URLs directing users to more guidance, for example a page on your website that gives more detailed explanation about how resources may be used
- the standard image or logo for the licence, for example a Creative Commons licence logo (https://creativecommons.org/about/downloads/)
- the name or identity of the licensor, for example your organisation.

These are some examples of licence and rights statements:

- 'Image licence: CC BY.'
- 'Unless otherwise stated, the text and images in this document are licensed under CC BY.'
- 'This image is licensed with a CC BY licence [URL].'

- 'This video may be used under the terms of the Creative Commons Attribution 4.0 International Licence [URL].'
- 'This metadata is in the public domain and may be freely used and reused.'
- 'Copyrighted work available under Creative Commons Attribution [URL].'
- 'Images on this page may be used under CC BY-NC-SA unless otherwise stated.'
- 'This image identified by National Library of Scotland is free from known copyright restrictions. Further guidance on use [URL] of public domain images.'
- 'Copyright © Gill Hamilton, 2017 with all rights reserved.'

Guidance for those using open resources

Not everyone who uses an organisations' open resources understands about open licensing, so it is important to publish short, clear, jargon-free guidance on how resources may be used, and what is expected of the person who uses them. The best place to provide this advice is likely to be on your organisation's website, where it is accessible to everyone, and you can link to it from your licence statements. It is common for organisations to have a web page or section explaining about copyright and intellectual property rights. This information should either be extended or a new web page created to include guidance on openly licensed resources.

The guidance should proactively encourage users to use open resources, explaining initially and positively how they may use material, before going on to outline how they should comply with licence terms, including any restrictions or limitations. As most users do not understand licensing in detail, they are unlikely to understand how to cite or provide attribution appropriately. Therefore, it may be helpful to consider including advice about this.

For example, you might explain a CC BY licensed digital resource in the following way:

You may freely use, change and republish works that are labelled CC BY for any purpose, including for commercial purposes, as long as you acknowledge [name of creator]. Find out more about CC BY [URL to Creative Commons CC BY page].

When citing our digital resources please include the title of the work and its URL, [name of the creator] and reference to the licence. For example:
'Queensferry cantilever from end of Hawes Pier, http://digital.nls.uk/74570380, National Library of Scotland, licensed under CC BY.'

For CC BY-NC-SA you might explain:

- You may freely use, change and republish works that are labelled CC BY-NC-SA for any non-commercial purpose as long as you acknowledge [name of creator] and re-publish any outputs you create using the same licence, CC BY-NC-SA. You may not use CC BY-NC-SA works commercially. If you wish to do so, please contact [contact details].
- When citing our digital resources please include the title of the work and its URL, [name of creator], and reference to the licence. For example:
  'SD36, http://maps.nls.uk/view/91739363, National Library of Scotland, licensed under CC BY-NC-SA.'

For public domain works, consider asking users to provide attribution even though this is not a mandatory requirement. You can still request attribution, or reference to provenance, without making this a requirement, for example:

You may freely use, change and republish works that are labelled Public Domain for any purpose, including commercial use, without restriction. We would be grateful if you would acknowledge [name of creator] as the original publisher so others know where to find this work. More about the public domain [URL to public domain information].

Tools and resources

Search tools to find openly licensed resources

With the open movement having become mainstream and openly licensed materials commonplace, many search engines and media hosting services incorporate search functionality that can filter search results to open resources only. With the help of the repositories and aggregators that host open resources, it is now easier than ever to find open licensed content.

Bing

Microsoft Bing's image search (www.bing.com/images) has an option to filter search results by licence including: 'all Creative Commons', 'free to share and use', 'free to share and use commercially', 'free to modify, share and use' and 'free to modify, share and use commercially'.

Creative Commons

The Creative Commons search tool (http://search.creativecommons.org/) searches services such as Europeana, Flickr, Google, New York Public Library, Open Clip Art, SoundCloud and Wikimedia Commons for Creative Commons or other openly licensed material. It sends the appropriate search syntax for retrieving open content to each selected service, so users do not have to learn how to construct a search for open content in each individual service. In 2017 Creative Commons is testing a new search prototype: https://ccsearch.creativecommons.org.

Foter

Foter (http://foter.com/) is a service that searches Flickr for Creative Commons licensed images. The Foter search results can then be further refined by selecting either 'commercial use' or 'non-commercial use'.

Google Advanced Search

Google Advanced Search has an option for filtering searches on particular usage rights.[3] When applied the filter searches for resources that are in the public domain, or have Creative Commons or similar open licences. Search options include: 'not filtered by licence', 'free to use or share', 'free to use or share even commercially', 'free to use share or modify' and 'free to use share or modify even commercially'. The advanced search on usage rights options can be used with the standard Google Search (www.google.com/advanced_search) or Google Image Search (www.google.com/advanced_image_search).

Repositories and aggregators of open resources

The Digital Public Library of America

The Digital Public Library of America (DPLA; https://dp.la/), like Europeana, is an aggregation service that gives access to more than 15 million resources from more than 2000 organisations across the US. While the DPLA search does not currently have a filter for open licensed content, many of the contributors are federal organisations whose content is made open as a requirement of US legislation. By refining searches to federal institutions, such as The National Archive and the Library of Congress, it is easily possible to identify open licensed resources. Other US organisations that openly license their resources, such as the New York Public Library, can be found through DPLA.

Europeana

Europeana (www.europeana.eu/) provides access to more than 30 million openly licensed image, sound, video, text and 3D resources by aggregating metadata associated with resources from cultural heritage organisations across Europe. When searching Europeana there are options to further refine rights statement searches by filtering on a combination of nine open licence options. The size and definition of many of the images on Europeana are high quality.

Flickr

The image and video-hosting site Flickr (www.flickr.com/search/) has options for filtering searches by licence including: 'any licence', 'any Creative Commons', 'commercial use allowed', 'modifications allowed', 'commercial use and modifications allowed', 'no known copyright restrictions' and 'US government works'. The licence filter can be used in combination with other advanced search features, such as limiting the search to videos only. On Flickr Commons (www.flickr.com/commons) more than 100 cultural heritage organisations from around the world have contributed millions of images from their collections under a 'no known copyright restriction' statement.

Free Music Archive

The music hosting service Free Music Archive (http://freemusicarchive.org/search/) contains over 100,000 openly licensed audio tracks. Its advanced search provides filtering on all variations of Creative Commons licences.

The HathiTrust Digital Library

The HathiTrust Digital Library (www.hathitrust.org/) is a partnership organisation that hosts a digital repository for the preservation of both public domain and in-copyright bibliographic works. It includes digitised content from many universities and public organisations in the United States, whose collections were digitised either in-house or in collaboration with Internet Archive, Google or Microsoft. The HathiTrust catalogue clearly states in its search results whether a resource is openly licensed (full view) or is restricted due to copyright or other reasons (limited view).

Internet Archive

Internet Archive (https://www.archive.org/) is a vast collection of archived websites, digital and digitised content, much of which is openly licensed.[4]

Search results can be filtered to show only open content, although this functionality is somewhat complex because it requires the use of the Archive's search syntax and an understanding of Creative Commons licence abbreviations. Fortunately, Internet Archive supplies some helpful guidance with preset searches.[5] Common searches for Internet Archive open resources might include:

- licenseurl:(http*publicdomain*) – only public domain resources
- licenseurl:(http*by*) – only Creative Commons Attribution (CC BY)
- licenseurl:(http*by-nc-sa*) – only Creative Commons Attribution, NonCommercial, ShareAlike (CC BY-NC-SA).

The searches can be combined using standard Boolean operators, for instance:

- licenseurl:(http*publicdomain*) OR licenseurl:(http*by*) – returns all resources licensed as public domain or Creative Commons Attribution (CC BY)
- (licenseurl:(http*publicdomain*) OR licenseurl:(http*by*)) AND hamsters – returns all resources licensed as public domain or Creative Commons Attribution (CC BY) that include the term 'hamsters'.

When building complex searches it may be helpful to use the advanced search function of the archive (https://archive.org/advancedsearch.php), which includes extensive help.

OpenStreetMap

For cartographic content the openly licensed mapping service OpenStreetMap (www.openstreetmap.org/copyright) licenses its data under an Open Data Commons Open Database Licence, and use and reuse of imagery and map tiles under CC BY.

SoundCloud

Similarly, SoundCloud (https://soundcloud.com/search/sounds), the audio hosting service, has a licence option in its advanced search that enables the following filtering options: 'modify commercially', 'to use commercially' and 'to share'.

Vimeo

Searches on Vimeo (https://vimeo.com/), another popular video-hosting service that includes much high quality, professional video content, can be filtered by a range of Creative Commons licences.

Wikimedia Commons

Wikimedia Commons (https://commons.wikimedia.org/wiki/Main_Page), also known as WikiCommons, is a repository of more than 38 million freely licensed images, sound, video and other media files. It was originally established as an archive of resources to support Wikimedia Foundation projects such as Wikipedia, but the wider use of Commons resources has always been encouraged. At a minimum Wikimedia Commons requires that resources are licensed with a CC BY-SA licence, although many are in the public domain. The Commons search function is not particularly sophisticated. However, all of its resources are discoverable either via Google Search or Google Image Search.

YouTube

The Google-owned video-hosting service YouTube (www.youtube.com/) has several filter options that become available after initiating a search. One of these filters is Creative Commons, which limits the search to videos with a Creative Commons licence or which are in the public domain. There are many videos on YouTube explaining how to find, use and reuse Creative Commons videos (use search statement 'find Creative Commons YouTube').

Reverse image lookup services

Reverse image lookup services are useful tools for finding the location of images on the web. In general they can be helpful when trying to gather information about an image, such as its creator or provider, when attempting to source a high-resolution version of an image, or when trying to find images that are similar to each other. These tools can also be used to monitor and track use of your own resources, whether for gathering metrics and information on their use and reuse, and their distribution across the global web, or for identifying and investigating misuse or licence infringement.

These services work by taking an image file or location (commonly a URL), processing the image using sophisticated algorithms originating from the computer vision industry, comparing the image with other similarly processed images in a database and, assuming matches are found, providing the user with a list of locations for the image on the web. Several of the large search engine companies (Google, Bing, Yandex) offer reverse image lookup facilities, as do other specialised companies including TinEye, PicMatch and Reverse Image Search. Two of the most popular services are Google Images and TinEye.

Google Images

Google Images (https://images.google.com/) is the largest index of images on the web and has several ways to reverse lookup. On the Google Images search site users can paste an image URL, drag and drop an image from a computer or a web page, upload an image from a computer, or if using a Chrome or Firefox browser right-click on an image and select 'Search Google with this image'. When Google processes an image search it automatically adds text to the query to refine the results, and users can subsequently change the text to further improve the refinement. The results include web pages that match the image and other images that are visually similar.

TinEye

TinEye (www.tineye.com/) has more than 17 billion images in its index and the service can be searched by URL, dragging and dropping images, or uploading files. TinEye also has plugins for major web browsers. TinEye has several useful functions that go beyond what Google Images currently offers, including: sorting images by Best Match, Most Changed and Biggest Image, and filtering by collection (which can help identify if an image is held on major services like Flickr and Wikimedia Commons). The Compare tool allows comparison of two images to see if changes have been made. This is particularly useful when used in conjunction with the 'Most Changed' sort option and can help determine how images have been modified. The service is free for non-commercial use and there are paid options for high volume use or image upload, tracking and reporting services.

If reverse image lookup tools are being used to monitor and track your organisation's resources on the web, it is worth bearing in mind that any search is unlikely to be entirely comprehensive. Search engines can, in general, only process what is published on the public, open web. Images that are held in the deep web, the area of the web where data is held in databases (such as library or museum catalogues) or is encrypted, are unlikely to be indexed by search engines, and are therefore difficult to discover and track.

Attribution resources and tools

One of the common requirements of openly licensed resources is that attribution must be given to the creator. All Creative Commons licences, except for the CC0 waiver, for example, require attribution under the 'BY' element. Students, teachers and academics are probably comfortable with providing citations, but attribution can be complex and confusing for others. Fortunately, there is guidance on how best to provide attribution and some tools that can help generate citations automatically.

Creative Commons

Creative Commons has a straightforward, best practice guide for providing attribution at https://wiki.creativecommons.org/wiki/Best_practices_for_attribution. It advises that all attributions should include at a minimum the title of the original work, the author of that work, the source of the work (its location or URL) and the licence assigned to the work. It also outlines how to give attribution when a work has been modified. For example, to attribute the above mentioned Creative Commons best practice document, an appropriate citation in a printed or offline document would be:

> 'Best practices for attribution' by Creative Commons at
> https://wiki.creativecommons.org/wiki/Best_practices_for_attribution is
> licensed under CC BY 4.0 https://creativecommons.org/licenses/by/4.0/

In an electronic document the title 'Best practices for attribution' would contain the hyperlink to the location and similarly the licence text 'CC BY 4.0' would hyperlink to the Creative Commons licence.

If, for example, I were to modify the Creative Commons' 'Best practices for attribution' document my attribution for an offline document would be:

> 'Best practice for attribution: guidance for GLAMs' by Gill Hamilton at
> [URL] is licensed under CC BY 4.0
> https://creativecommons.org/licenses/by/4.0/. It is a derivative work of 'Best
> practices for attribution' by Creative Commons at [URL] licensed under CC
> BY 4.0 https://creativecommons.org/licenses/by/4.0/.

Creative Commons Australia

Creative Commons Australia has produced detailed guidance about attribution that is clear, easy to follow and has excellent examples that guide the reader through the process of attribution. It is particularly helpful in the area of understanding and attributing derivative works as well as the originals from which works have been derived. See http://creativecommons.org.au/materials/attribution.pdf.

Foter

Foter has a helpful infographic that explains Creative Commons licensing and includes advice about how to give attribution for photographs. Foter also has an attribution tool that automatically generates an attribution statement in HTML for each image being viewed. See http://foter.com/blog/how-to-attribute-creative-commons-photos/.

Open Attribution Builder from Open Washington

The Open Attribution Builder from Open Washington (www.openwa.org/open-attrib-builder/) is a useful tool for generating attribution statements in HTML. It is a simple form-based service allowing input of the title of the work, the author, the location or URL, and the licence and licence version assigned to the work.

ImageCodr

ImageCodr (www.imagecodr.org/) is a tool that automatically generates an HTML attribution statement from the URL of any Flickr image that has a Creative Commons licence.

Tools to distribute openly licensed content

Organisations usually publish their openly licensed resources on their website where, unless they are hosted in a database or catalogue, they are available to search engines for indexing. The resources can then be discoverable via those search engines. Consideration should also be given to distributing open resources to large, popular, third party websites and resources as well, such as Wikimedia Commons, the Internet Archive, Europeana, Flickr and YouTube, in order to increase visibility and use. Most of these services have tools for loading content individually or in bulk.

Wikimedia Commons

Wikimedia Commons (WikiCommons) is the image, video and audio repository for all Wikimedia Foundation projects. Content loaded onto the

Commons may be reused in articles on Wikipedia, where reach is likely to be significant, and may also be reused outwith Wikimedia projects since people often source openly licensed resources from the Commons. There are several tools that are useful for loading content on to Wikimedia Commons:

- The Upload Wizard assists with the process of loading, describing, categorising and licensing files. It can be helpful if individual or a small number of files are to be loaded. See https://commons.wikimedia.org/wiki/Special:UploadWizard.
- The GLAMwiki Toolset is specifically designed to help cultural heritage organisations bulk load their resources and associated metadata. It requires that the metadata describing the resources be in XML format and therefore some modest technical knowledge is necessary. See https://commons.wikimedia.org/wiki/Commons:GLAMwiki_Toolset.
- There are other upload tools, including for desktop and mobile devices and for transferring open resources to the Commons from services such as the Internet Archive and Flickr. See https://commons.wikimedia.org/wiki/Commons:Upload_tools.

Internet Archive

The digital library service Internet Archive (https://archive.org/) has developed a bulk loading tool that like the Wikimedia Commons Upload Wizard helps load, describe, categorise and license files. The tool is straightforward to use, requires no particular technical expertise, and includes options to preset metadata for multiple uploads. A third party tool, IAS3API, which enables bulk loading content, requires technical knowledge.[6]

Europeana

Europeana aggregates metadata from European cultural heritage organisations through Europeana Collections, Exhibitions Foyer and other services. Cultural organisations can contribute their metadata by becoming a member of Europeana and are required to submit their metadata under the CC0 licence or waiver. In general, Europeana can either harvest or collect metadata directly from organisations using protocols such as the Open Archives Initiative Protocol for Metadata Harvesting (OAI-PMH) or ftp, or indirectly via one of its aggregation partners. See https://ec.europa.eu/digital-single-market/en/europeana-european-digital-library-all.

Flickr

There are several different ways that content can be uploaded to the image and video-hosting service Flickr (www.flickr.com):

- The Flickr Uploadr tool (www.flickr.com/tools/) for desktops for both Windows and MacOS can bulk load and process thousands of images and associated metadata, though it requires a Flickr Pro account costing approximately US$50 for two years. Uploadr is easy to use and requires no technical expertise.
- The Flickr apps for iOS and Android allow images to be uploaded from mobile devices easily. Multiple images can be uploaded, although a limited amount of metadata can accompany the images. Metadata updates, such as adding the author and links back to the original resource at an organisation's website, have to be added by hand after the image is uploaded.
- Flickr also has a powerful application programming interface (API) that allows programmatic interaction with Flickr accounts, content and search services (www.flickr.com/services/api/). The API has sophisticated functions for uploading images along with descriptive metadata. Technical expertise is required to use the API.

YouTube

For distributing audio and video resources to YouTube (https://www.youtube.com/) there are three upload methods:

- The standard YouTube Upload function allows uploading of one video or audio file at a time. After the file is loaded metadata can be added. The uploader is simple to use and useful if only small numbers of audio or video files are being loaded. See https://support.google.com/youtube/answer/3077589.
- The Package uploader allows bulk uploading of multiple video and audio files and their associated metadata, which must be held in a separate spreadsheet or XML file – YouTube supply templates that can be used to help prepare metadata in the correct format. The Package uploader is easy to use and requires little to no technical expertise. See https://support.google.com/youtube/answer/3077589.
- Like Flickr, YouTube has a powerful suite of APIs that can be used programmatically to bulk upload video and audio files and supply

appropriate metadata fields. Technical expertise is required to use the API. See https://developers.google.com/youtube/v3/guides/uploading_a_video.

Notes

1   Creative Commons Australia, Licence Elements, factsheet, 19 June 2009, http://creativecommons.org.au/materials/factsheets/cc-licences.pdf.
2   Copyright User, Public Domain, 2017, http://copyrightuser.org/topics/public-domain/.
3   Google Help, Find Free-to-use Images, 2017, https://support.google.com/websearch/answer/29508?hl=en.
4   Goel, V., Defining Web pages, Web Sites and Web Captures, Internet Archive, 23 October 2016, https://blog.archive.org/2016/10/23/defining-web-pages-web-sites-and-web-captures/.
5   Internet Archive, Frequently Asked Questions, 2017, https://archive.org/about/faqs.php.
6   GitHub, Internet Archive S3 API: documentation, 2017, https://github.com/vmbrasseur/IAS3API#internet-archive-s3-api-documentation.

Chapter 14

Conclusion

We hope we have given you sufficient justification for and practical examples of open licensing so that you are now in a position to consider making the case for its implementation in your organisation.

You have seen how the open movement has evolved since the 1960s into a variety of sub-movements, such as open data, open educational resources, and open government and that unbeknownst to most people, openness is in fact at the centre of our modern digital lives. We have hopefully brought clarity and understanding to the legal and statutory frameworks that surround intellectual property rights, explained the threshold of originality uncertainty that exists in UK law and described the public domain, licensing terminology and open licensing frameworks. In acknowledging that cultural organisations are open by nature and having armed yourself with an awareness of the regulations and the benefits and risks associated with open licences, you should be well placed to advance the case for *open* in your organisation.

The case studies demonstrate some of the different approaches that organisations take to being open. Sometimes these approaches are ad hoc and opportunistic, as in the early days of open licensing at National Library of Scotland, sometimes they are part of a specific project, such as the Wikimedian in Residence at National Library of Wales, sometimes they address challenging intellectual property issues head on, such as at the Wellcome Library, and sometimes they grow up in response to government calls to open public information, as in the case of the British Library's open metadata strategy. The University of Edinburgh shows how policy, training and awareness can support the development and distribution of open educational resources, and warns us against the dangers of copyright debt when failing to record attribution in teaching materials. Statens Museum for Kunst shows us how even when starting small, the impact of open can be huge both in cultural and social terms, and can go on to drive further open licensing and engagement. The experiences of Newcastle Libraries show that allowing people to use and reuse even a modest amount of content openly can be a powerful demonstration to managers that concerns regarding risks are unlikely to be warranted. All of these organisations, however they started out with openness, show that when open licensing is adopted, formalised, and working as a business as usual practice, benefits are realised and many initial concerns over risks start to melt away.

Finally, we have left you with some guidance on how to practically implement and record your open licensing decisions, as well as some pointers, guidelines, and tools to help you find and attribute open resources.

One final piece of advice. Our experience, and that of some of our case study contributors, tells us that you may encounter hurdles when making the case for or implementing open licensing. This may be in attempting to resolve complex intellectual property rights issues, trying to convince resistant colleagues that open is both viable and likely to become inevitable, or in addressing senior managers' concerns over loss of control and income generation. In these moments of frustration, do not become disheartened; sometimes it just takes time, sometimes it requires a redoubling of your efforts, sometimes it requires different approaches. The important thing is to push on and keep your eyes on the prize. That prize is contributing to a better world, with free and open access to knowledge for everyone, made possible and perpetuated by forward-looking, inclusive, modern and relevant cultural heritage organisations.

We wish you the very best in all your open licensing endeavours.

Index